camouflage patterns

100 royalty free eps and jpeg files

A DEX BOOK

Copyright © DesignEXchange Company Limited.

Published in Japan in 2002 by
DesignEXchange Company Limited.
Nakameguro GS Dai2 Building
2-9-35 Kamimeguro
Meguro-ku Tokyo 153-0051 Japan
e-mail:intl@dex.ne.jp
http://www.dex.ne.jp

ISBN 4-900852-90-2

Publisher: Masanori Omae
Art Direction: NENDO GRAPHIXXX
Design: C*2
Book Design: Katsuya Moriizumi
English Translation: Richard J. Sadowsky + BABEL K.K.
Production Assistant: Isshin Hirata
Production: Rico Komanoya

Manufactured in Japan by DaiNippon Printing Company Limited.

First Printing, 2002

Introduction

【 camouflage patterns 】 をお買い上げありがとうございます。
この迷彩パターン集はロイヤリティ（使用権）フリーになっておりますので、グラフィックデザイン、インターネット、3Dのマッピング、デスクトップパターンなど幅広くご利用いただけます。収録形式はEPSファイル形式と、JPEGファイル形式の2種類に分かれます。JPEGファイル形式は、縦幅が480ピクセルに設定されたパターンファイルを用意しました。
パターンの読み込み方法や、加工方法は、ご利用のアプリケーションソフトに準じます。御不明な点については、ご利用のアプリケーションソフトのマニュアルをお読みください。

EPSファイル形式
● EPSファイル形式の特長
このファイル形式のデータは、「Adobe Illustrator」などのグラフィックソフトを使うと、変形したり、色を変更するなどの編集が比較的簡単に出来ますが、写真のように色や明るさに濃淡〔階調〕がある画像には適していません。
Adobe社の技術であるPostScriptに対応しており、プロセス印刷用などの高解像度出力には、一般的にこの形式を用います。パターン線自体の切り離しや接合、オブジェクトの色の塗りや、変形など精密な加工が可能です。
Macintoshではかねてより一般的なファイル形式でしたが、最近ではWindowsでも「Microsoft Word」など一般的なアプリケーションや、「Adobe PageMaker」などのレイアウトソフトで使用できる環境が整いつつあります。
● 画像の解像度とカラーモードについて
EPSファイル形式は「解像度」や「カラーモード」にはあまり関係がありません。拡大縮小してもきれいに印刷出来ます。
● EPSファイル形式の大きさ（容量）について
EPS形式のファイルの容量は、画像ファイル全体の線や点の多さによって決まります。絵の大きさは関係しません。

JPEGファイル形式
● JPEGファイル形式の特長
小さな四角形の点＝ピクセル (pixel) を並べることにより「絵」を描画しますので、写真のように色や明るさに濃淡〔階調〕がある画像に適しています。「Adobe Photoshop」などのペイントソフトやフォトレタッチソフトと呼ばれるソフトウェアで加工や修正をすることが出来ます。PICT形式や、BMP形式と比べて保存時の圧縮効率が高いので、同じピクセル数の解像度でもファイル容量は小さくなります。
● 画像の解像度について
解像度は画像ファイルの精密さを表わす尺度で、1インチの直線に何個のピクセルが並んで入るかで決まります。「dpi」(dot per inchの略) という単位がつけられますが、72dpiの画像であれば1インチの直線に72個のピクセルが、それに対して300dpiでは300個のピクセルが並んでいることになり、約4倍の精密さを持っています。したがって、同じ大きさに印刷した場合では72dpiよりも300dpiの画像の方がはるかにきれいに印刷されます。このファイルでは、解像度は72dpiに設定されていますので、インターネットなどのデジタルの環境以外、例えば紙媒体などに利用する際には、パターンデータの解像度を上げなくてはいけません。（普通の紙の上で使われる解像度は300dpi〜350dpiです。)
● JPEGファイル形式の大きさ（容量）について
JPEG形式のファイルの容量は、画像ファイル全体のピクセル数と色数のほか、圧縮率によって決まります。圧縮率を高くしてファイル容量を小さくすると、画像が劣化します。

This collection of patterns is royalty-free and can be used for graphic design, web pages, 3D mapping, desktop patterns, etc. The data is provided in EPS and JPEG files. The JPEG files are pattern files with a height of 480 pixels.
For instructions on how to import or use, please consult the manual of the application being used. Other questions will also be answered by reading the manual.

The EPS File Format
● Features of the EPS File Format
This file format is suitable for use with a graphic program such as Adobe Illustrator that makes it possible to modify the pattern, change the colors, and perform other editing tasks rather easily. The format is not suitable for images that depend on gradients of color or brightness, such as photographic ones.
The format is compatible with Adobe's PostScript language, and is the format generally used for high-resolution output such as process printing. Precision processing can be done on this type of file, such as detaching or joining the pattern lines themselves, or change the fill color of an object.
The EPS file format has long been standard on the Macintosh, and has recently begun to be adopted in Windows applications--in general application such as Microsoft Word and layout software such as Adobe PageMaker.
● Image Resolution and Color Mode
Image resolution and color mode have little to do with the EPS file format. Enlarged or minimized, the file prints out just as cleanly.
● EPS File Format Size
The size of the EPS file will depend on the amount of lines and pixels in the image file as a whole. How large the picture appears is not a determining factor.

The JPEG File Format
● Features of the JPEG File Format
A JPEG image is formed of tiny square blocks known as pixels, so the format is suitable for images that depend on gradients of color or brightness, such as photos. The file can be modified, retouched or otherwise processed using Adobe Photoshop or other paint or retouching software. The format offers greater compression than a PICT or BMP file, making the JPEG file size smaller at the same pixel resolution.
● Image Resolution
Resolution is a measure indicating the level of detail of an image file determined by the number of pixels in one inch. The unit is known as "dpi" (dots per inch). At 72 dpi there are 72 pixels side by side along a straight one-inch line, while 300 dpi has 300 pixels, about four times the density or level of detail. Consequently, when printed at the same size, the 300 dpi image will print much more beautifully than the 72 dpi image. The resolution of these files is 72 dpi, so if they are to be used outside of a digital environment like the Internet, on paper for example, the resolution of the pattern data must be raised. (The standard resolution for paper is 300-350 dpi.)
● JPEG File Format Size
The size of the JPEG file will depend on the number of pixels and colors in the image file as a whole, as well as the compression rate. The greater the compression, the smaller the file size will be, but the more the image will be degraded.

Tips

このパターンは、Adobe Illustrator 5.0 J 以上のバージョンで使用できます。（Adobe Illustrator 日本語での動作確認済み）

パターンを使用する

あらかじめパターンで塗られた四角形オブジェクトをアートボードに配置したファイルをご用意しました。この中から塗りを適用したいオブジェクトを選んでお使いください。もしくは、ペイントパレットにパターンを登録したファイルをご用意していますので、Adobe Illustrator フォルダ内にあるグラデーションとパターンフォルダへ迷彩パターンを登録したファイルを保存し、ファイルを読み込んで使用してください。

アートワークファイル内でパターンを使用するには、ペイントパレットを使います。カスタムカラーやグラデーションの塗りつぶしと同じように、パターンは現在の書類と共に保存されます。Adobe Illustrator 7.0 J では、ツールパレットの塗りの四角形を直接オブジェクトにドラッグ＆ドロップすると、パターンの塗りが適用されます。

プログラムを起動したときに、頻繁に使うパターンが読み込まれるように起動用ファイルをカスタム化することもできます。

パターンを修正する （Adobe Illustrator 5.0 / 5.5 J）

既に作成したパターンを編集して、新しいパターンを作成したいときはパターンダイアログボックス内の［ペースト］オプションを使って、元のアートワークのコピーをアートワーク書類内にペーストします。

1. オブジェクトメニューから「パターン」を選び、パターンダイアログボックスを表示させます。
2. ペーストしたいパターン名を選んでクリックします。
3. ［ペースト］をクリックします。
4. ［OK］をクリックします。選択したパターンが、アートワーク書類内にペーストされます。この後、このパターンを編集し、新しいパターンとして定義することができます。
5. ペーストされたパターンを再編集します。
6. 調整したパターンを選択します。
7. オブジェクトメニューから「パターン」を選び、パターンダイアログボックスを表示させます。
8. 再定義するパターン名を選択します。
9. ［OK］をクリックします。

パターンを修正する （Adobe Illustrator 7.0 J）

1. アートワークの選択を全て解除します。
2. ウィンドウメニューから「スウォッチを表示」を選び、修正するパターンのスウォッチを選択します。
3. パターンスウォッチをアートワークにドラッグ＆ドロップします。
4. パターンを再編集します。
5. パターンを選択します。
6. Option キー（Macintosh）または、Alt キー（Windows）を押しながら、修正したパターンをスウォッチパレット上の古いパターンスウォッチ上にドラッグ＆ドロップします。スウォッチパレット上でパターンが置き換わり、開いている書類中の同じパターンが全て変更されます。

パターンをプレビュー、プリントする

書類設定ダイアログボックス内の［パターンをプレビュー、プリントする］オプションは、プレビューモードでパターンを画面上に表示します。［パターンをプレビュー、プリントする］オプションは、初期設定として選択されています。パターンをプレビュー、プリントしたくない場合は、このオプション解除をします。

These patterns require the use of Adobe Illustrator version 5.0J or later. (Confirmed to work properly with Adobe Illustrator version __J.)

Using the Patterns

These files contain square objects already painted with a pattern and placed on the Artboard. Choose the object upon which you wish to apply the fill. It is also possible to place the camouflage pattern files into the Gradient and Pattern folders within the Adobe Illustrator folder where they will be read in and become usable under the pattern files listed in the paint palette.

To use the patterns in an artwork file, use the paint palette. Patterns are saved with the current file in the same way as custom colors and gradient fills. In Adobe Illustrator 7.0J, the pattern fill is applied by dragging and dropping the tool palette's Fill square directly onto the object.

It is also possible to customize the start-up file so that frequently used patterns are read in automatically when launching the program.

Modifying a Pattern (Adobe Illustrator 5.0J/5.5J)

When you want to edit an existing pattern to create a new pattern, use the "paste" option within the pattern dialog box to paste a copy of the original artwork into the artwork file.

1. Choose "Pattern" from the Object menu to bring up the Pattern dialog box.
2. Choose the name of the pattern you want to paste in and click on it.
3. Click on "Paste."
4. Click "OK." The selected pattern will be pasted into the artwork file. The pattern can then be edited and defined as a new pattern.
5. Re-edit the pasted pattern.
6. Select the modified pattern.
7. Choose "Pattern" from the Object menu to bring up the Pattern dialog box.
8. Select the name of the pattern to be redefined.
9. Click "OK."

Modifying a Pattern (Adobe Illustrator 7.0J)

1. Delete all artwork.
2. Choose "Show Swatches" from the Window menu and choose the pattern swatch you wish to modify.
3. Drag and drop the pattern swatch onto the artwork.
4. Re-edit the pattern.
5. Choose the pattern.
6. While pressing and holding down the Option key (Macintosh) or the Alt key (Windows), drag and drop the modified pattern swatch onto the old pattern swatch on the swatch palette.

Pattern Previewing and Printing

The Preview & Print Pattern option in the file settings dialog box displays the pattern on the screen in preview mode. This option is selected as a preference. When this option is not desired, it can be turned off.

パターンを使った選択範囲の塗りつぶし（Adobe Photoshop 4.0J / 5.0 日本語版）
「塗りつぶし」コマンドを使って画像内の選択範囲をパターンで塗りつぶすことができます。この場合は、編集メニューの「パターンの定義」コマンドでパターンを定義しておく必要があります。パターンを新しく定義すると現在のパターンが置き換えられてしまうので、作成したパターンを再利用する場合は、パターンファイルの見本を保存します。この見本を使うとパターンを簡単に定義することができます。

選択範囲をパターンで塗りつぶすには
1. パターンとして使う画像を選択します（Commandキー＋Aキー）。
2. 編集メニューから［パターンの定義］を選択します。
3. 編集メニューから［塗りつぶし］を選択します。
4. 「使用」で「パターン」を選択し、「OK」をクリックします。

パターンオプション
「パターン」オプションを使うと、選択したパターンをスタンプツールでペイントできます。「パターン（調整あり）」オプションでは、ペイント操作を何度中断しても連続パターンを作成できます。「パターン（調整なし）」オプションでは、ペイント操作を中断して再開するたびに、スタンプポインタの中央からペイントが始まります。
スタンプツールの「パターン」オプションを使うには
1. パターンとして使う画像を選択します（Commandキー＋Aキー）。
2. 編集メニューから［パターンの定義］を選択します。
3. スタンプツールをダブルクリックしてオプションパレットを表示します。
4. 「パターン」オプションを選択します。
5. ドラッグしてパターンをペイントします。

Filling a Selected Area with a Pattern (Adobe Photoshop 4.0J/5.0J)
A selected area within the image can be filled with the pattern using the Fill command. To enable this it is necessary to define the pattern using the Define Pattern command in the Edit menu. Creating a new definition for a pattern will overwrite the current pattern, so to re-use the created pattern save it as a sample. Use this sample file to easily define patterns.

To fill a selected area with a pattern:
1. Choose the image that you wish to use as a pattern (Command-A).
2. Choose "Define Pattern" from the Edit menu.
3. Choose "Fill" from the Edit menu.
4. Choose "Pattern" from the Use pop-up menu, then click "OK."

The Pattern Option
Using the Pattern Option allows the selected pattern to be painted using the stamp tool. The Pattern (Aligned) Option can be used to paint a series of the defined pattern no matter how many times painting is interrupted. The painting starts at the center of the stamp pointer.

To use the stamp tool's Pattern Option:
1. Choose the image that you wish to use as a pattern (Command-A).
2. Choose "Define Pattern" from the Edit menu.
3. Double click the stamp tool to bring up the Option palette.
4. Choose "Pattern" option.
5. Drag to paint the pattern.

camouflage
patterns
No. 001

camouflage
patterns
No. 002

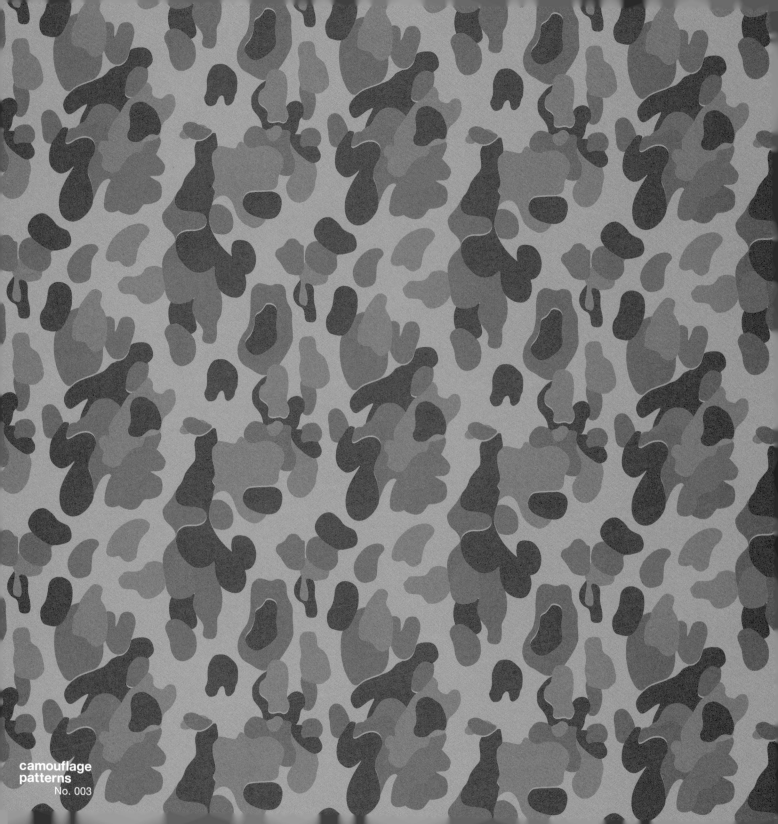

camouflage
patterns
No. 003

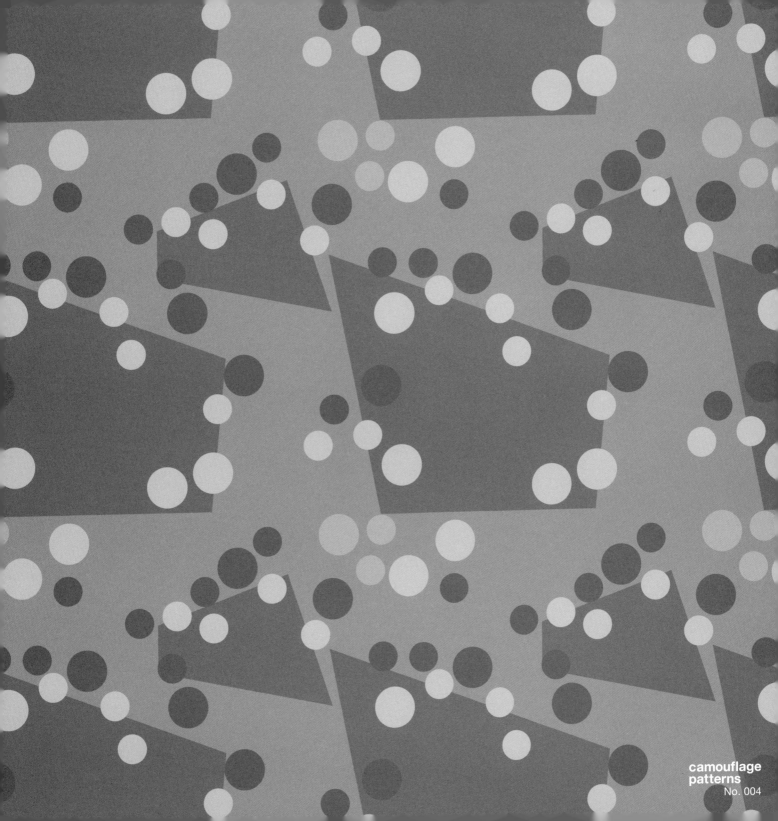

camouflage
patterns
No. 005

camouflage
patterns
No. 007

camouflage
patterns
No. 008

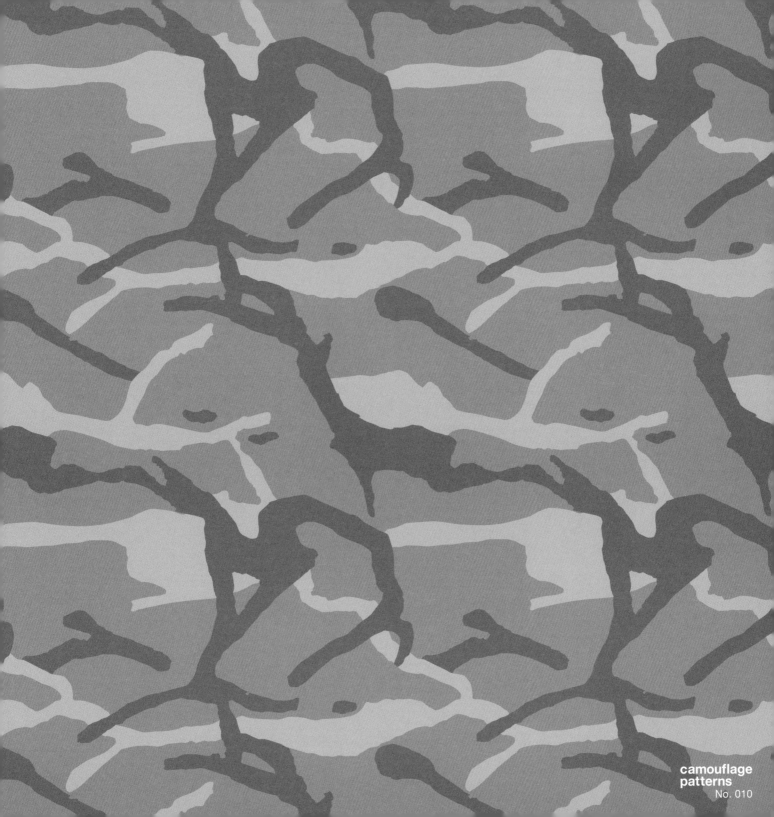

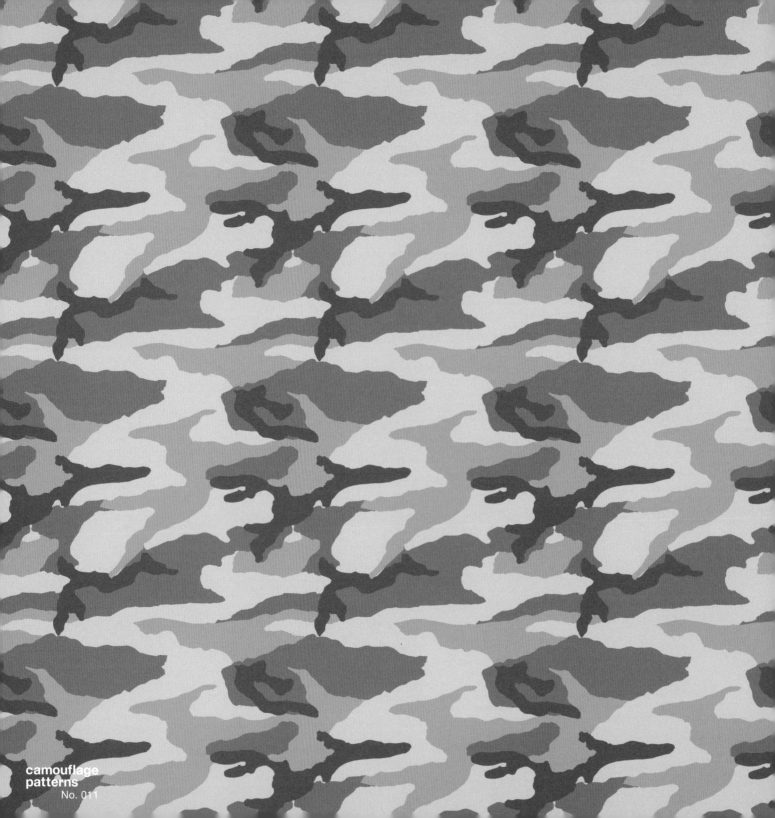

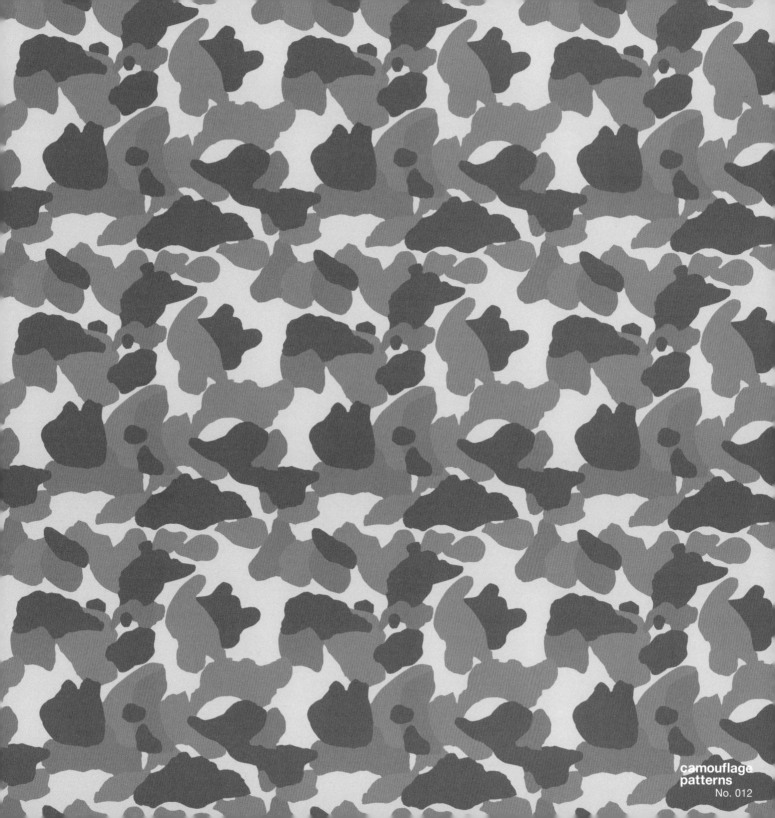

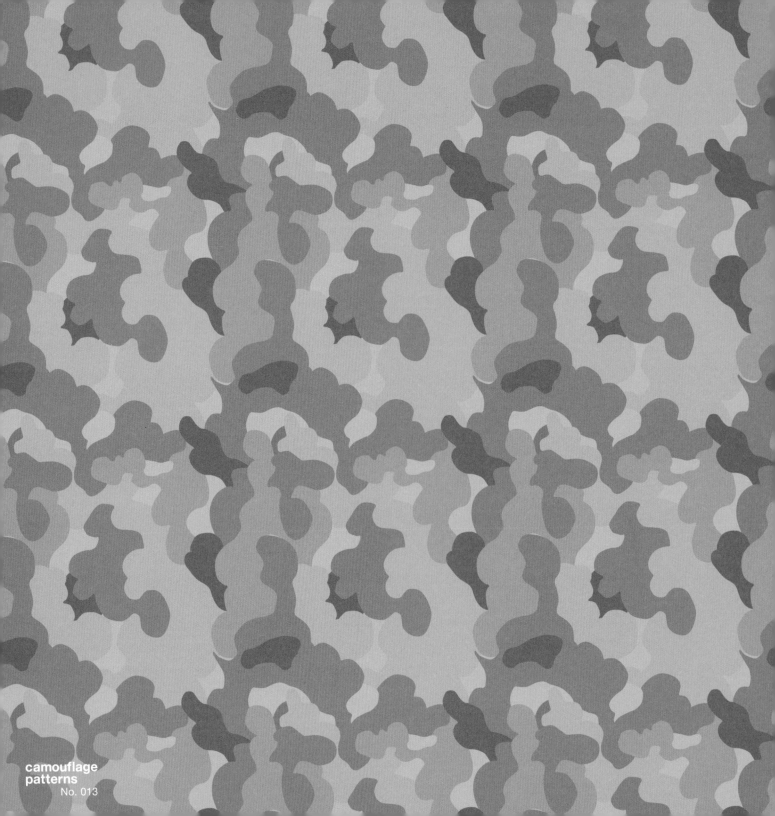

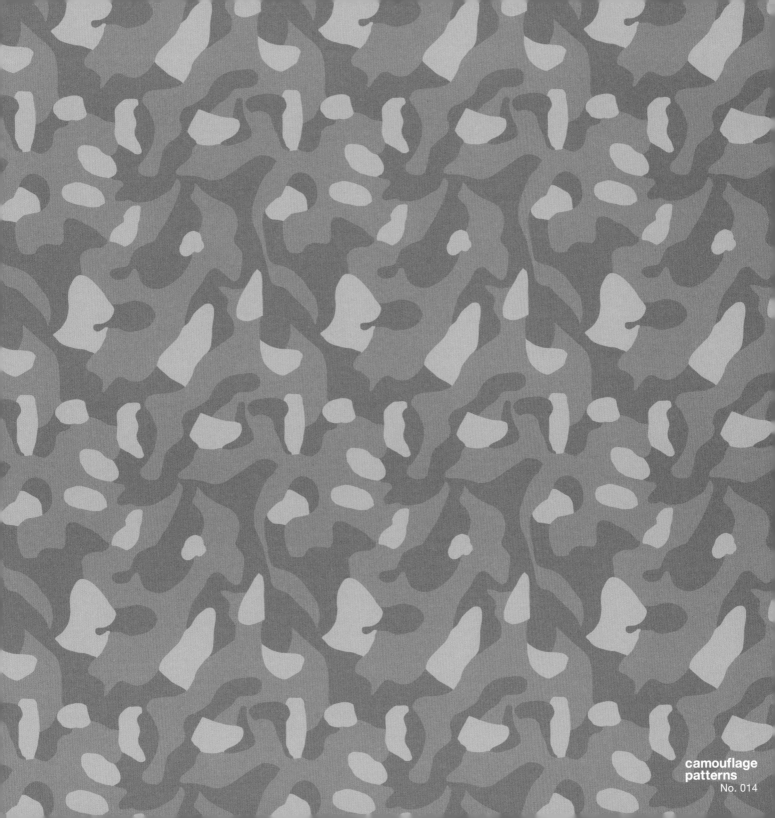

camouflage
patterns
No. 014

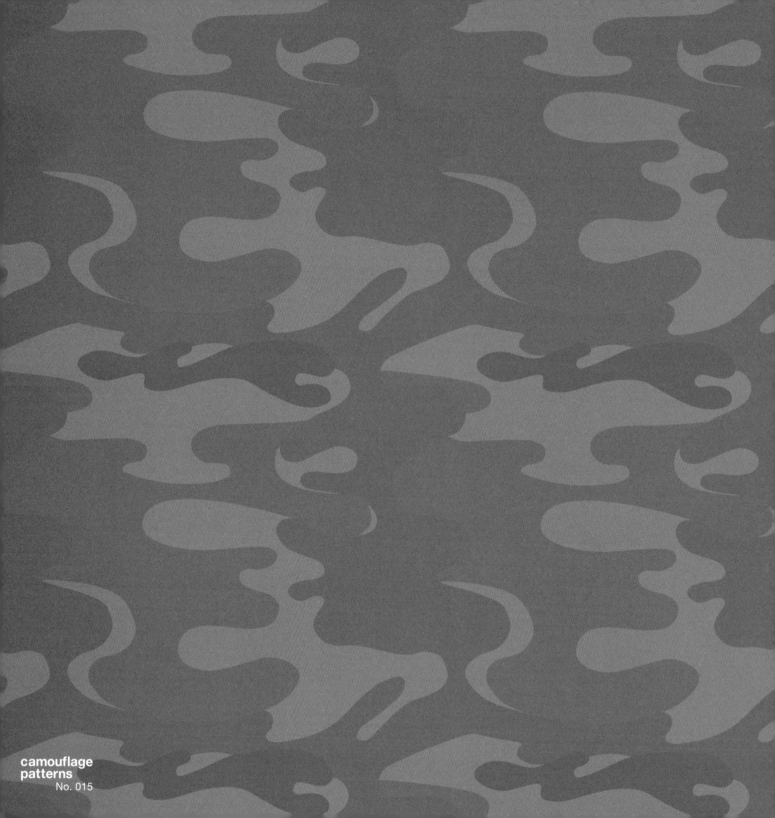

camouflage
patterns
No. 015

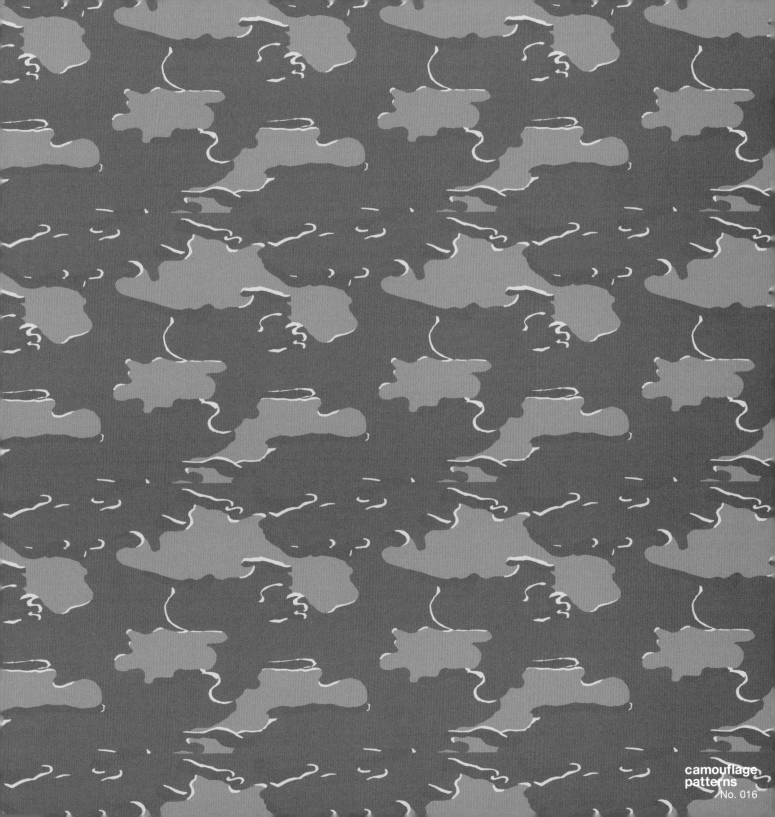

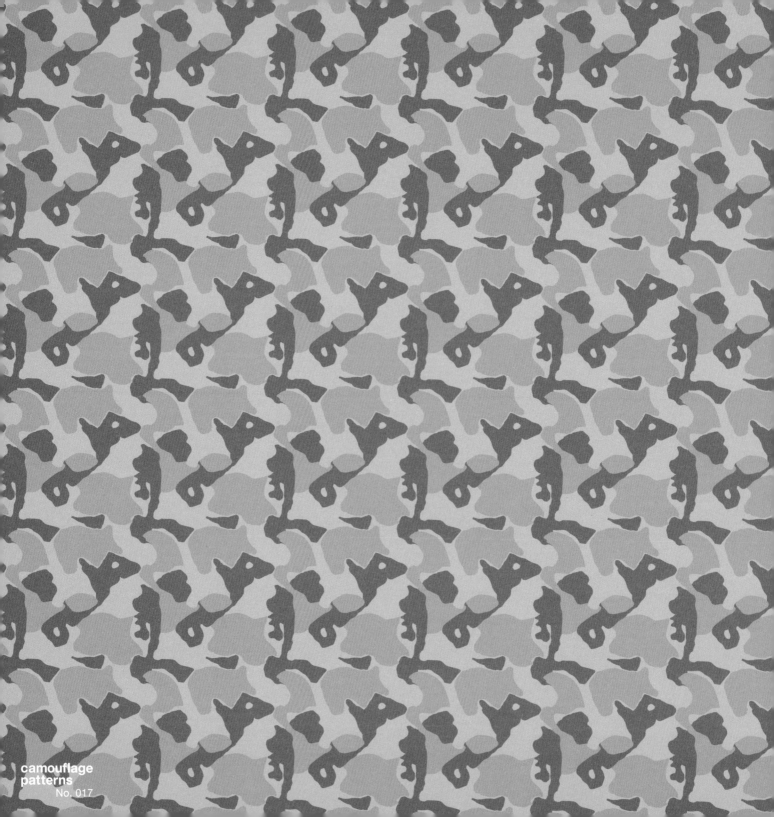

camouflage
patterns
No. 018

camouflage
patterns
No. 019

camouflage
patterns
No. 020

camouflage
patterns
No. 021

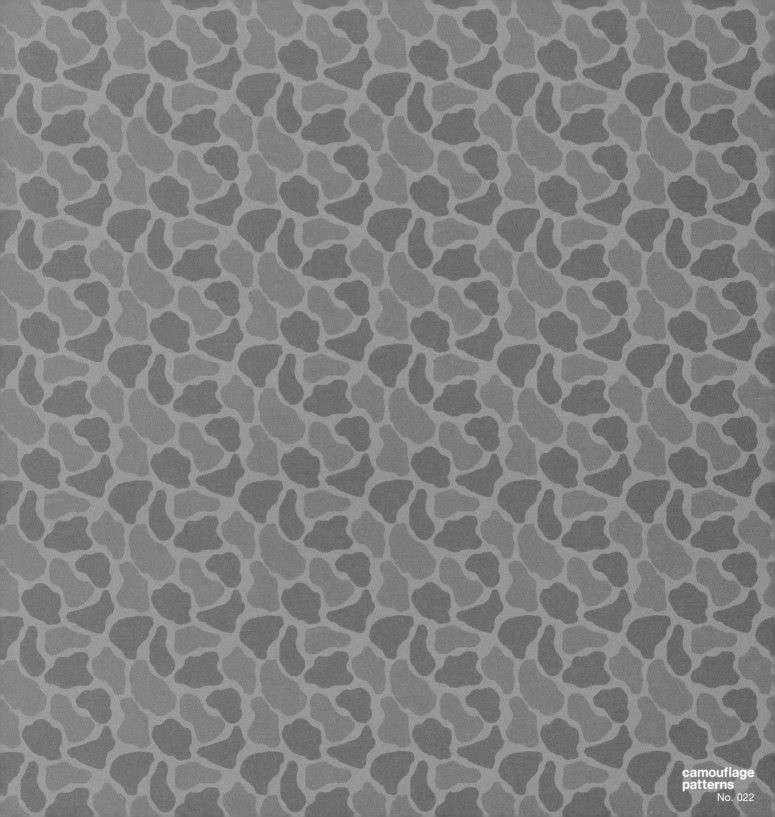

camouflage
patterns
No. 022

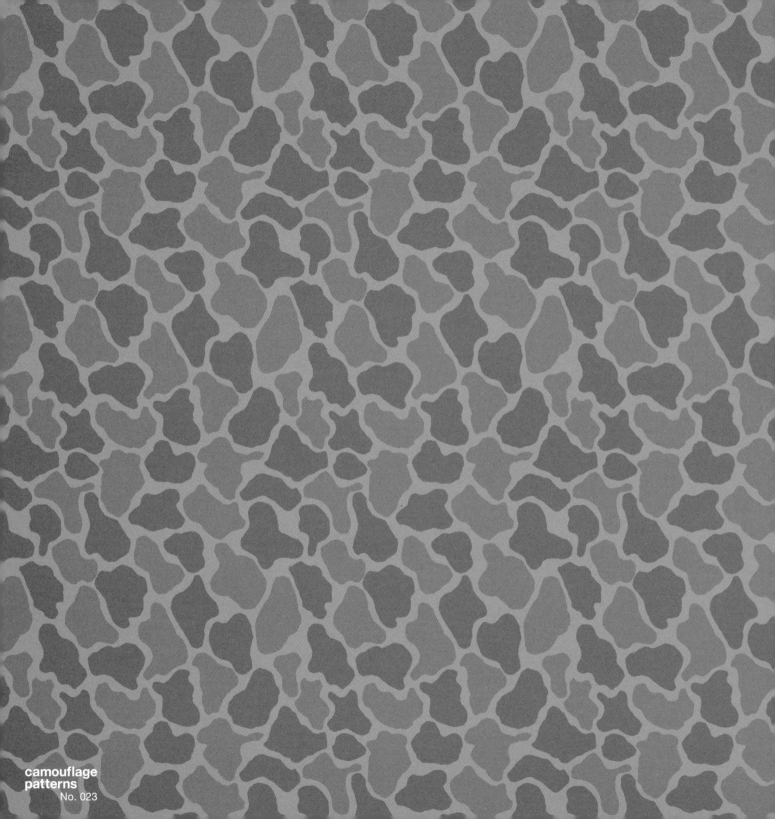

camouflage
patterns
No. 023

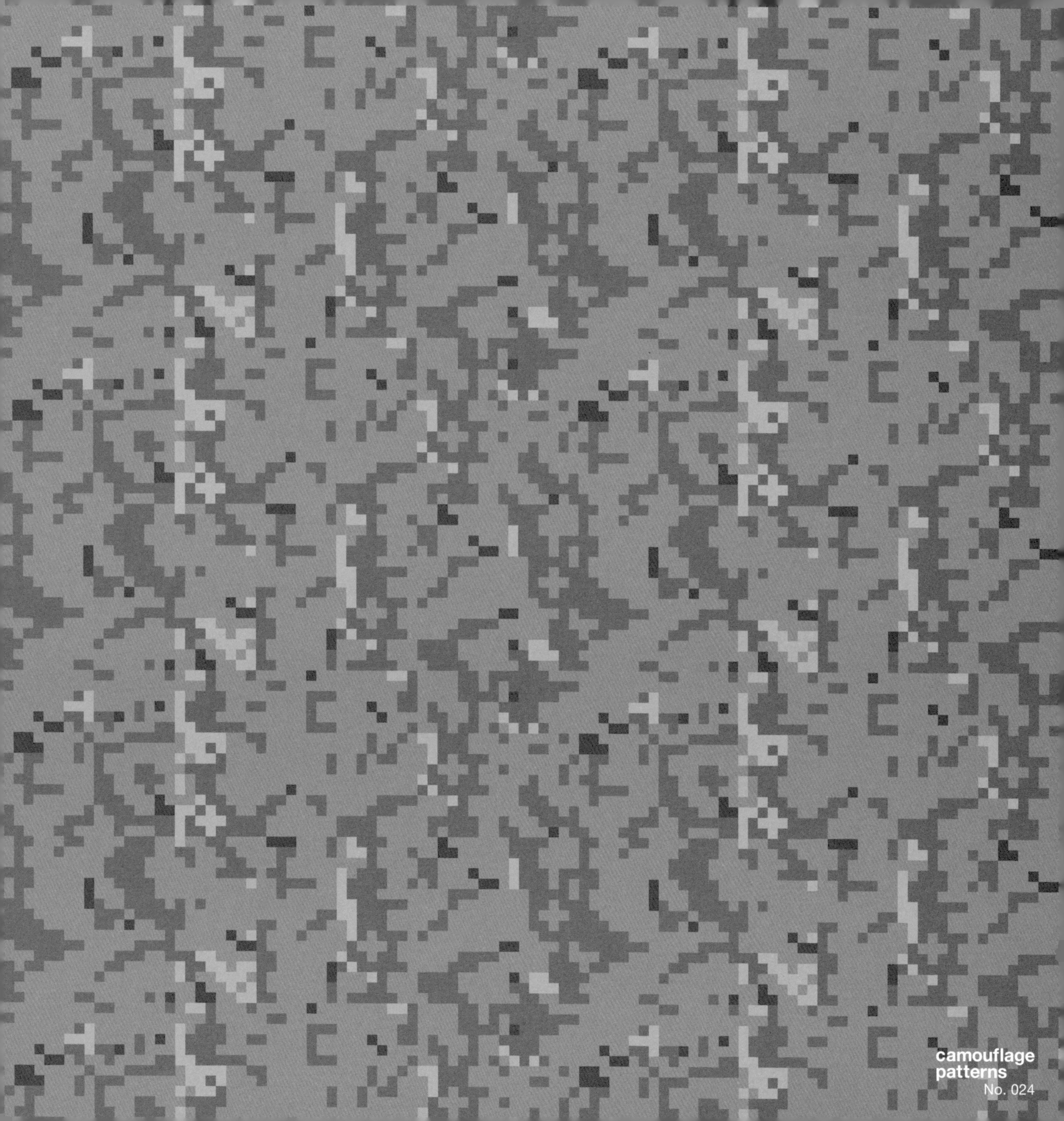

camouflage
patterns
No. 024

camouflage
patterns
No. 025

camouflage
patterns
No. 026

camouflage
patterns
No. 027

camouflage
patterns
No. 028

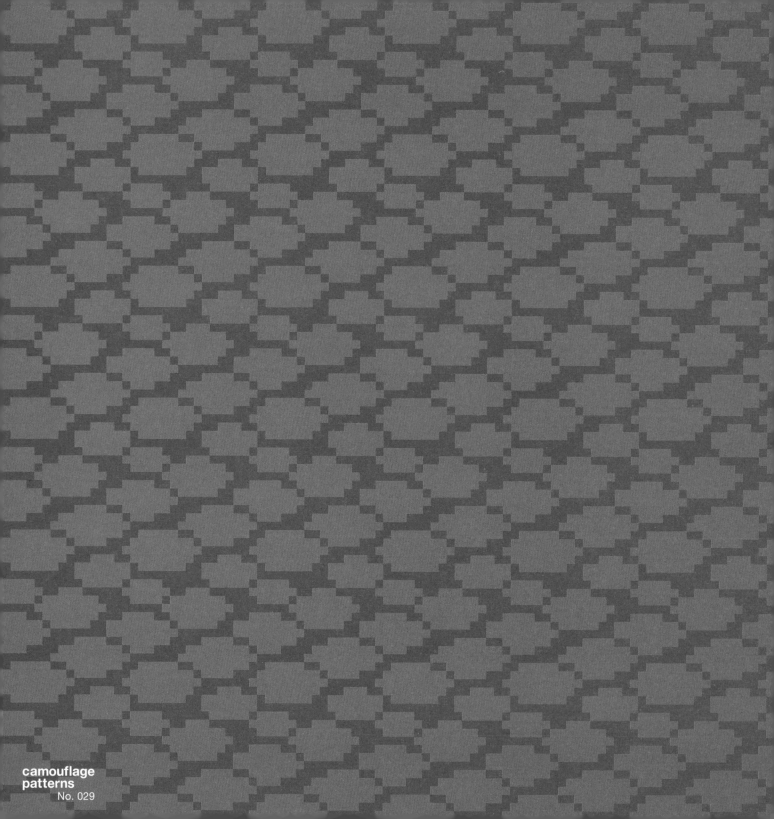

camouflage
patterns
No. 029

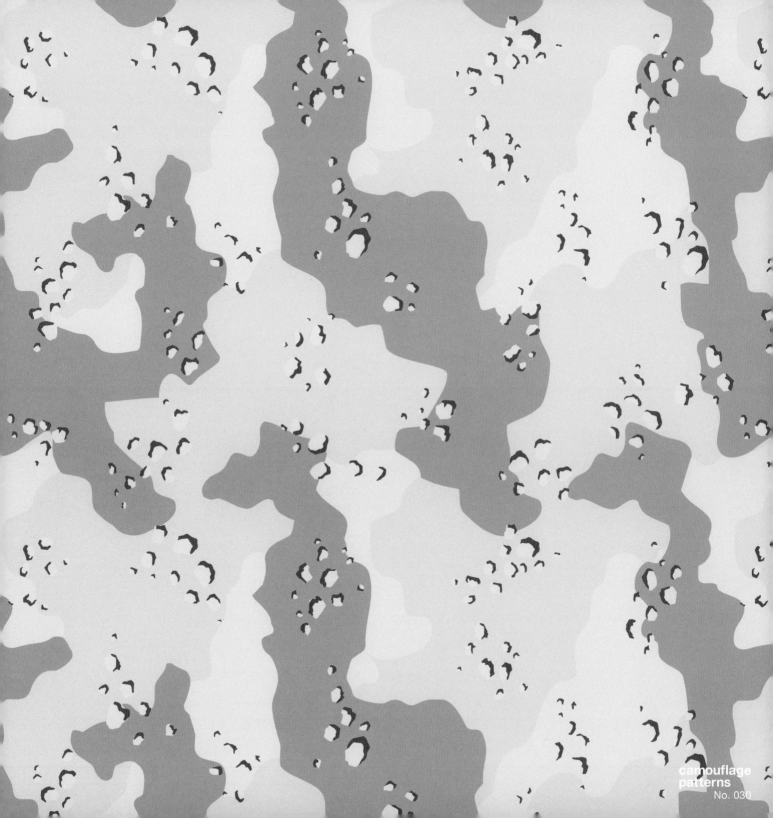

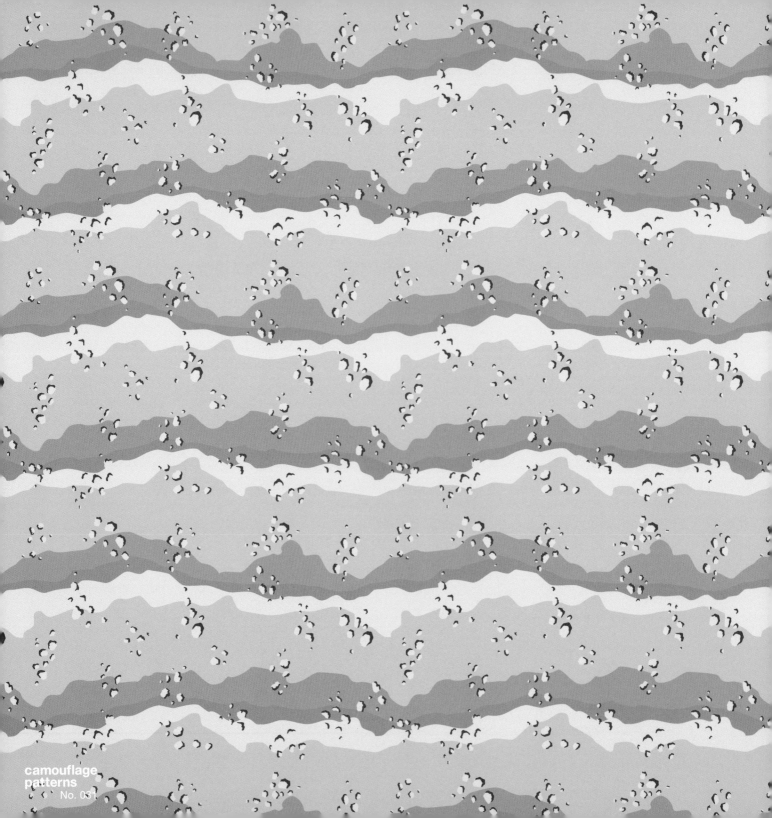

camouflage
patterns
No. 031

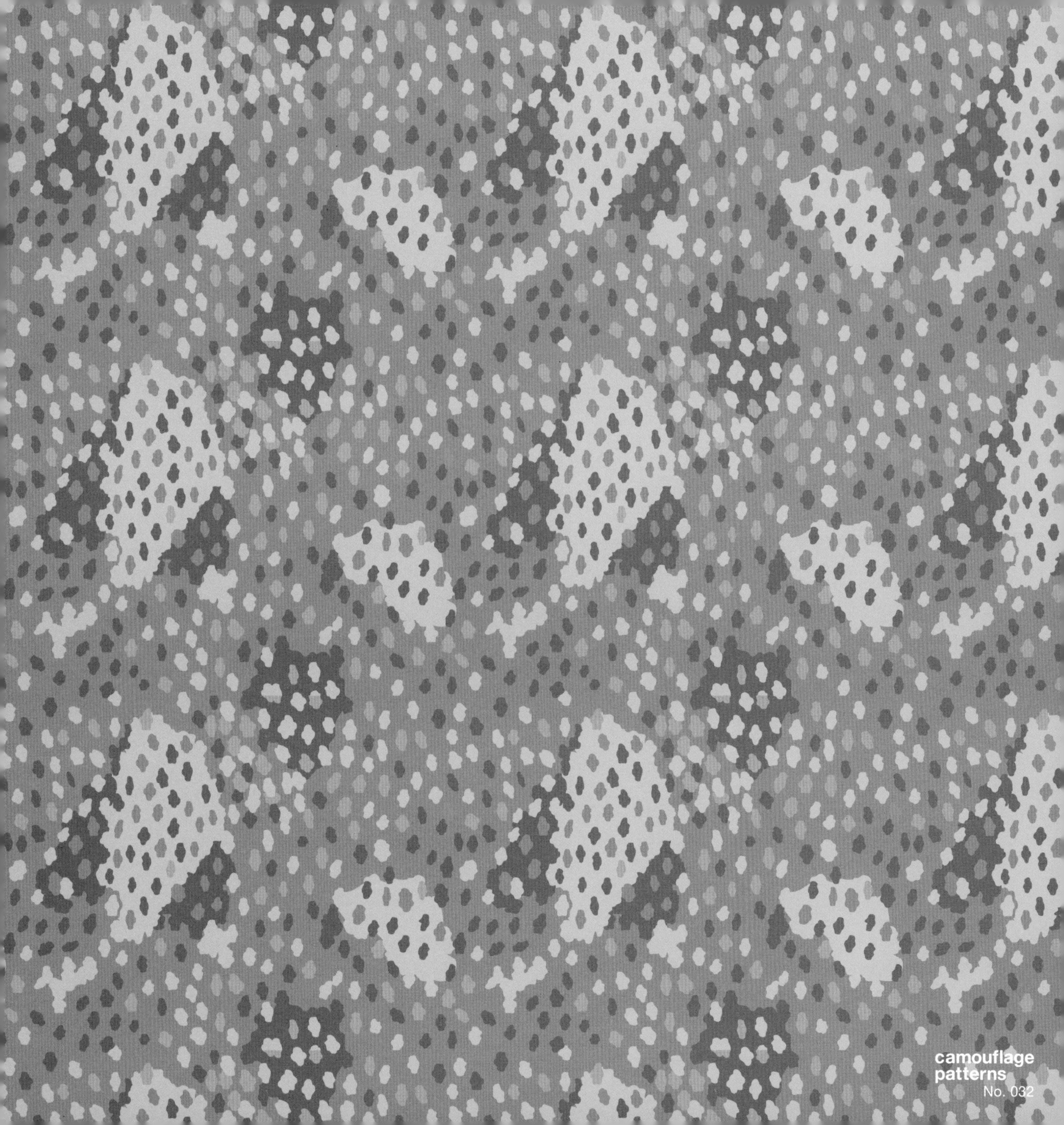

camouflage
patterns
No. 032

camouflage
patterns
No. 033

camouflage
patterns
No. 034

camouflage
patterns
No. 035

camouflage
patterns
No. 036

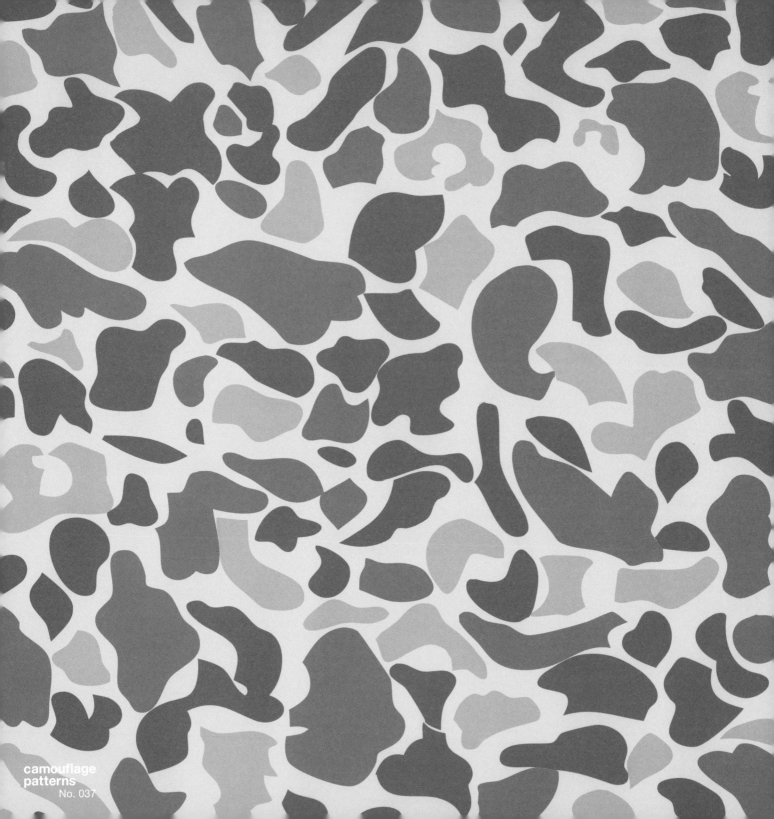

camouflage
patterns
No. 037

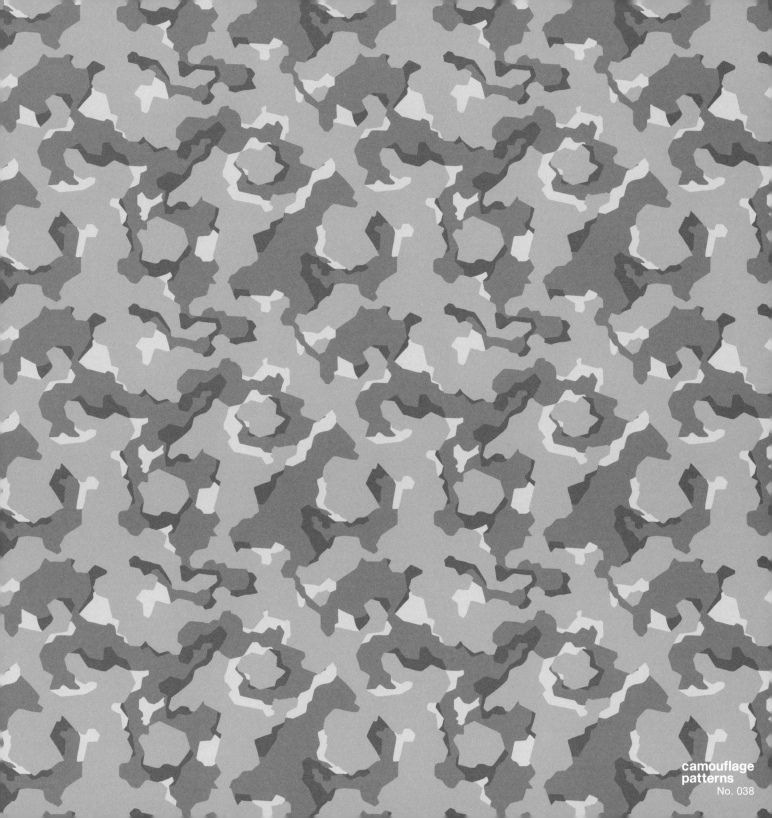

camouflage
patterns
No. 038

camouflage
patterns
No. 040

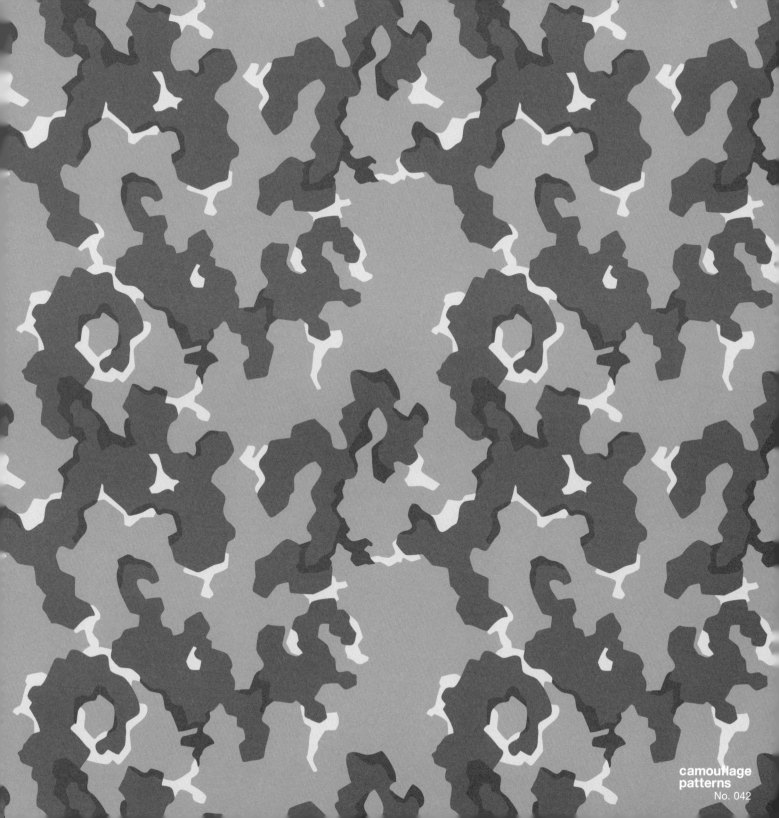

camouflage
patterns
No. 042

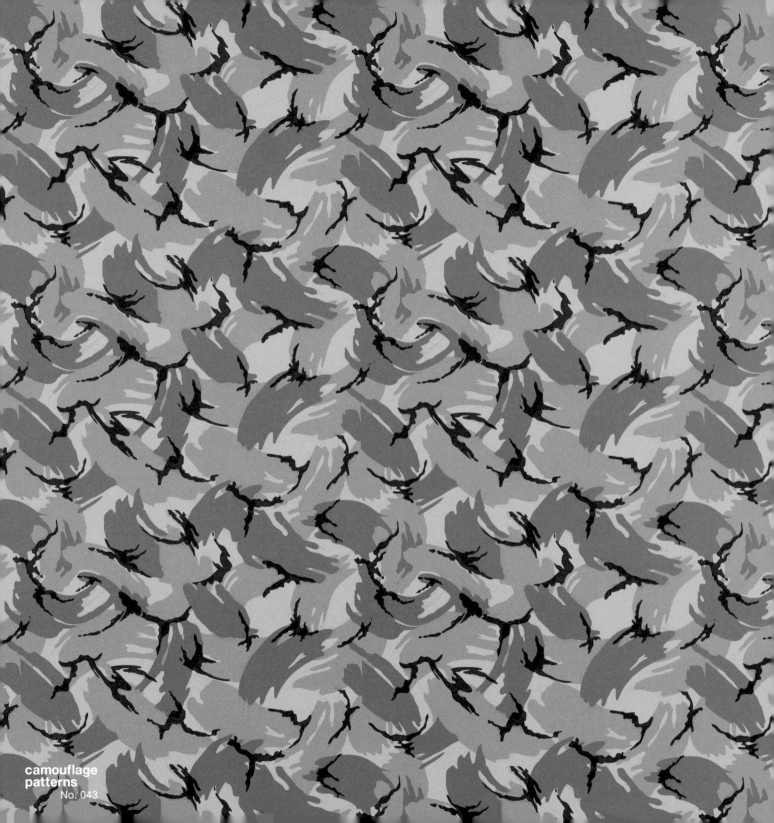

camouflage
patterns
No. 043

camouflage
patterns
No. 045

camouflage
patterns
No. 047

camouflage
patterns
No. 048

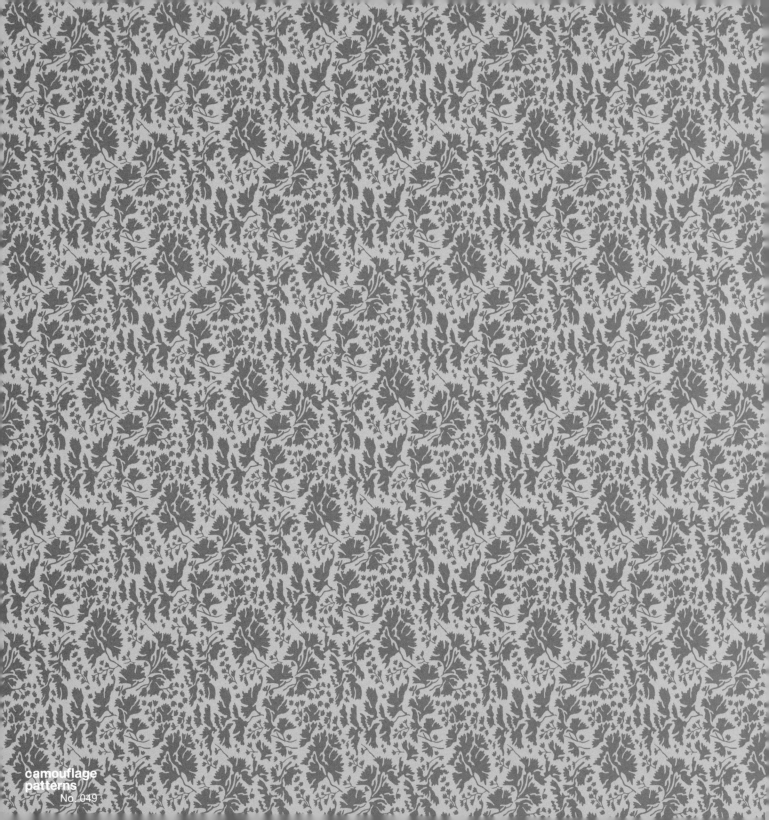

camouflage
patterns
No. 050

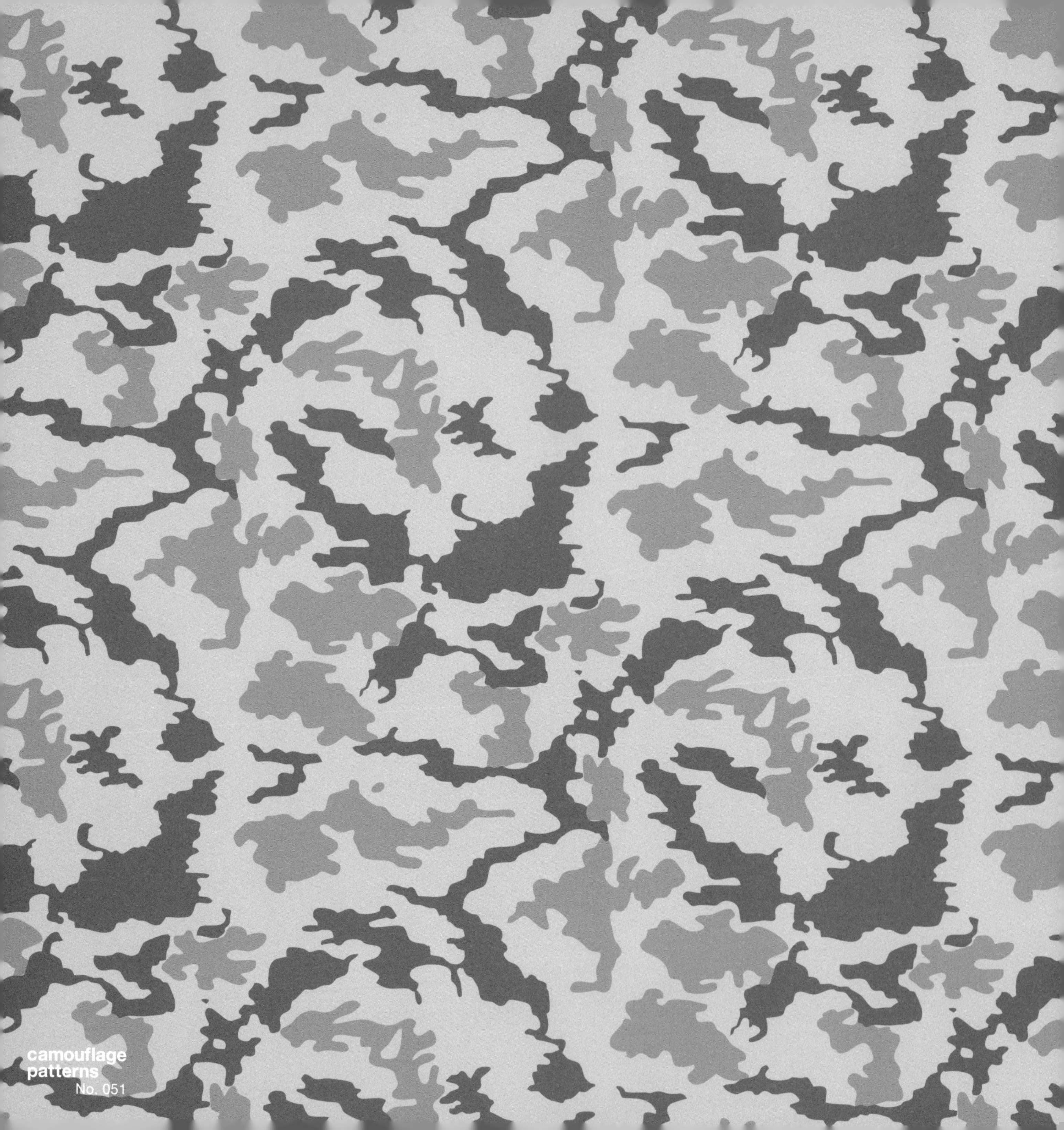

camouflage
patterns
No. 051

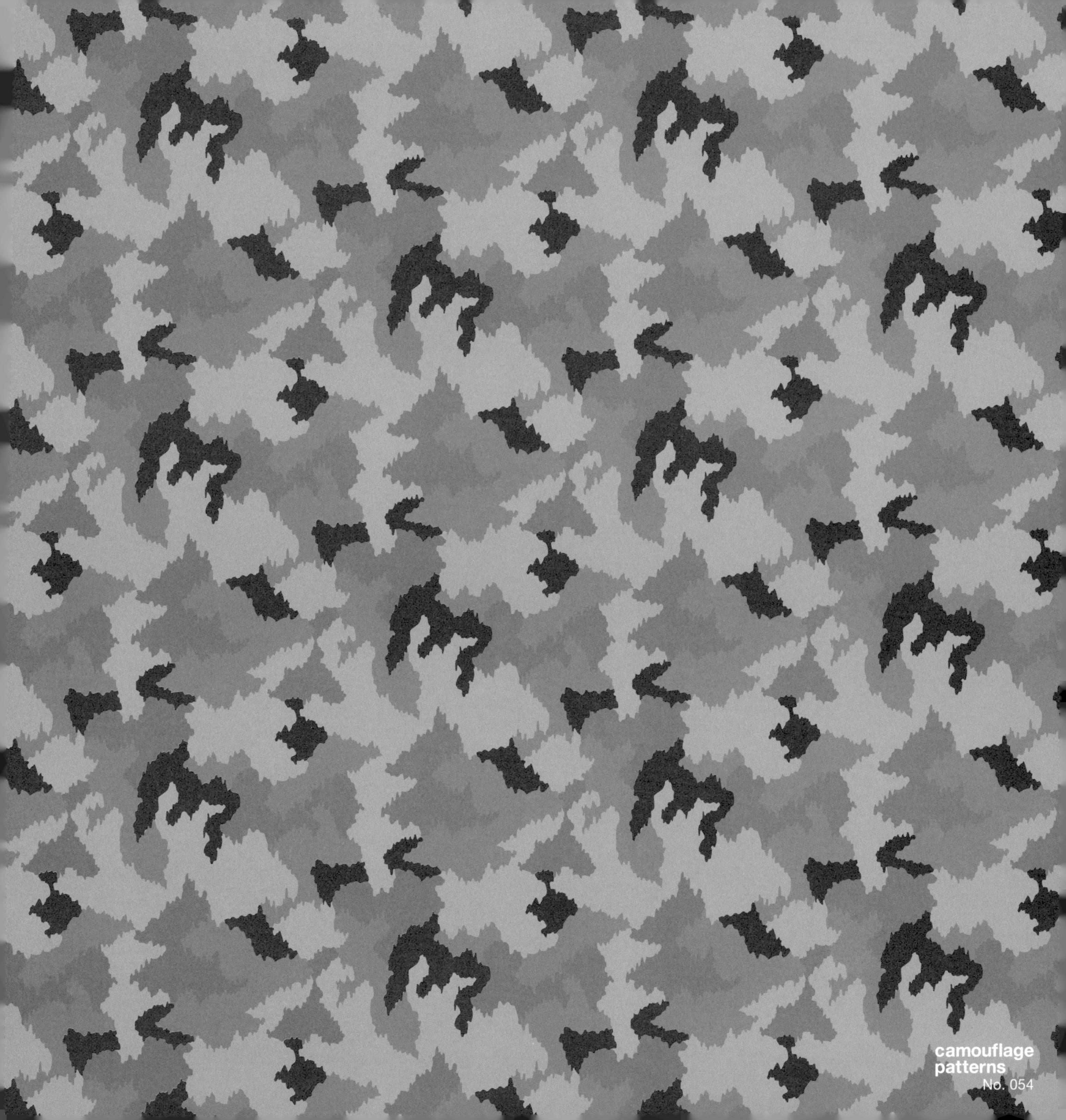
camouflage
patterns
No. 054

camouflage
patterns
No. 055

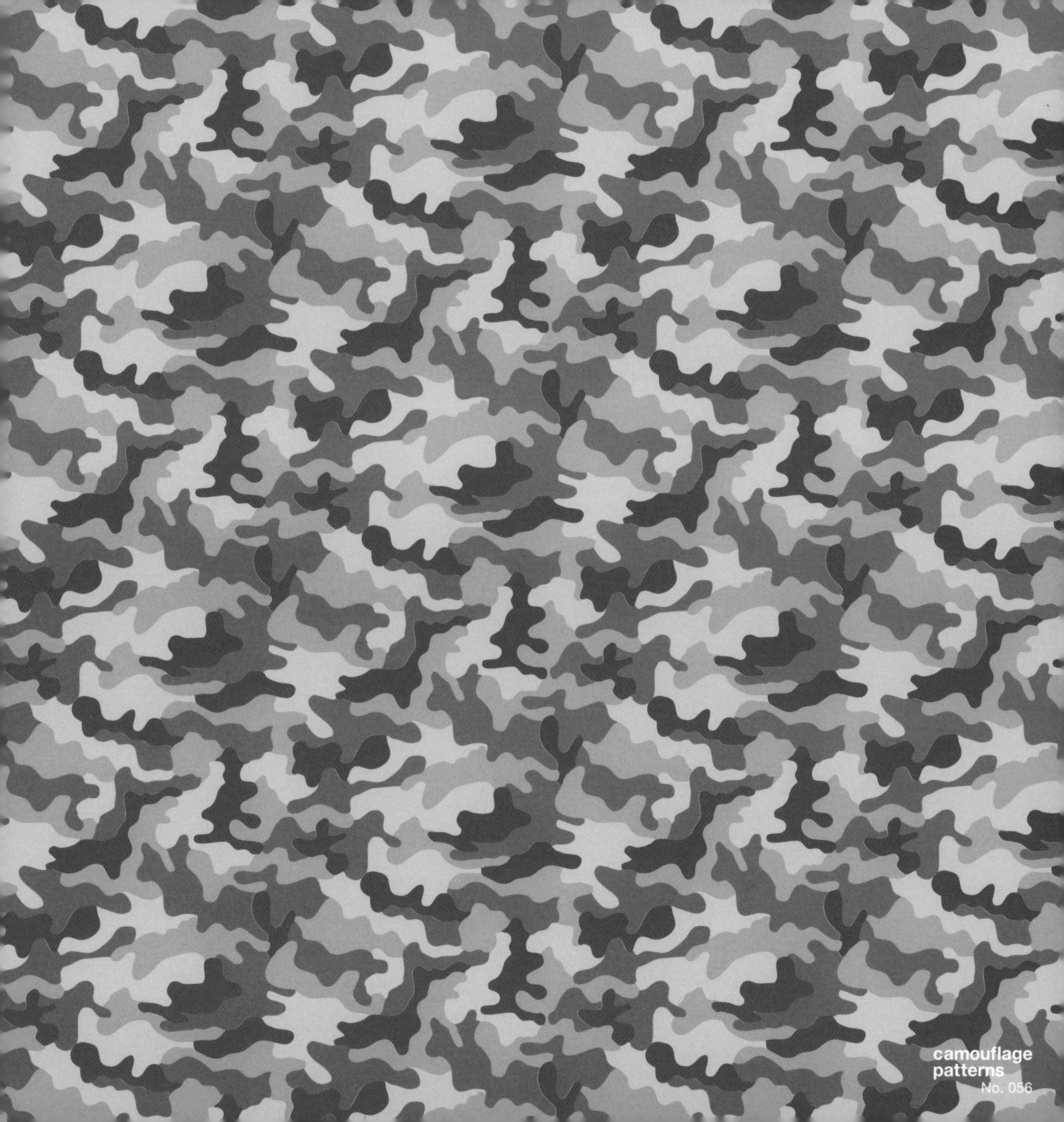

camouflage
patterns
No. 056

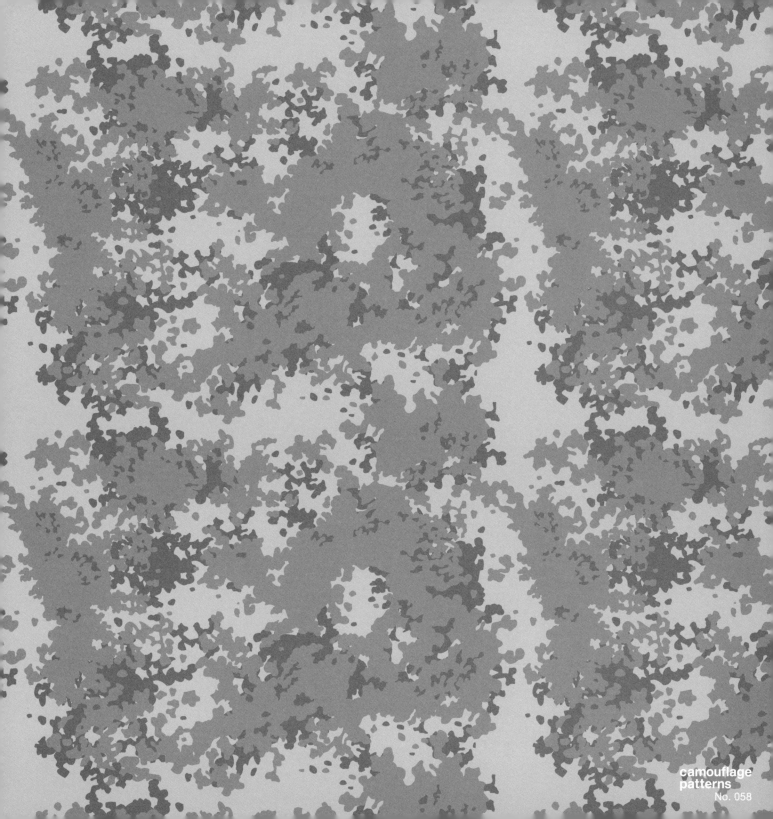

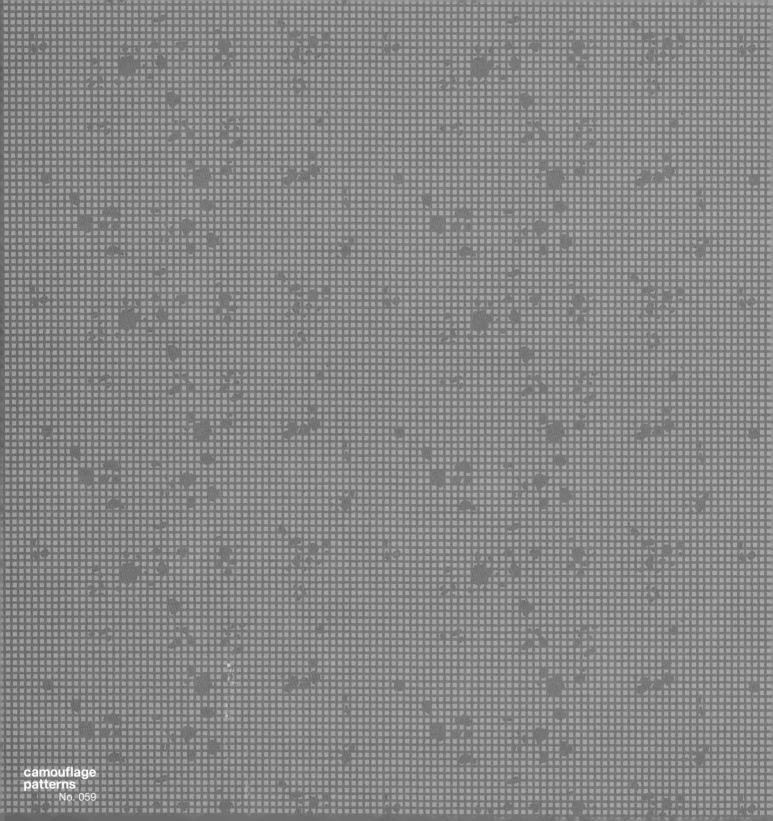

camouflage
patterns
No. 059

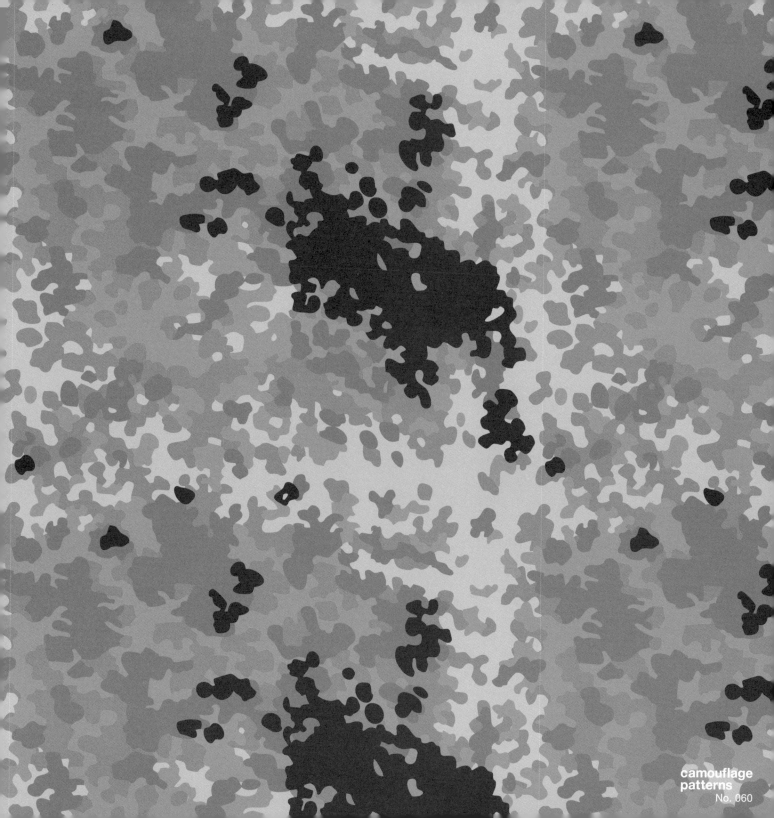

camouflage
patterns
No. 060

camouflage
patterns
No. 061

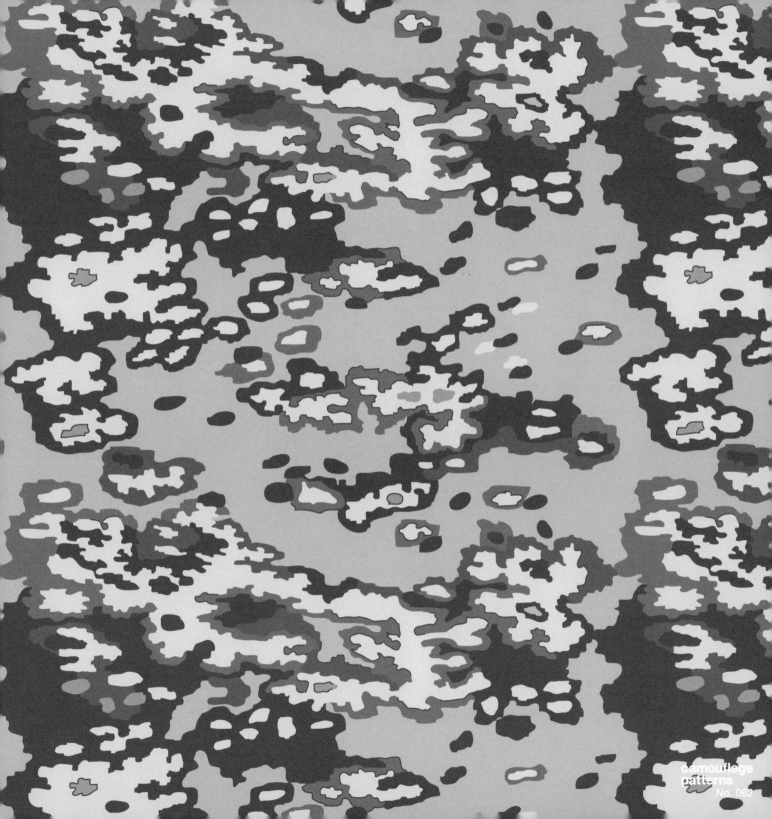

camouflage
patterns
No. 063

camouflage
patterns
No. 064

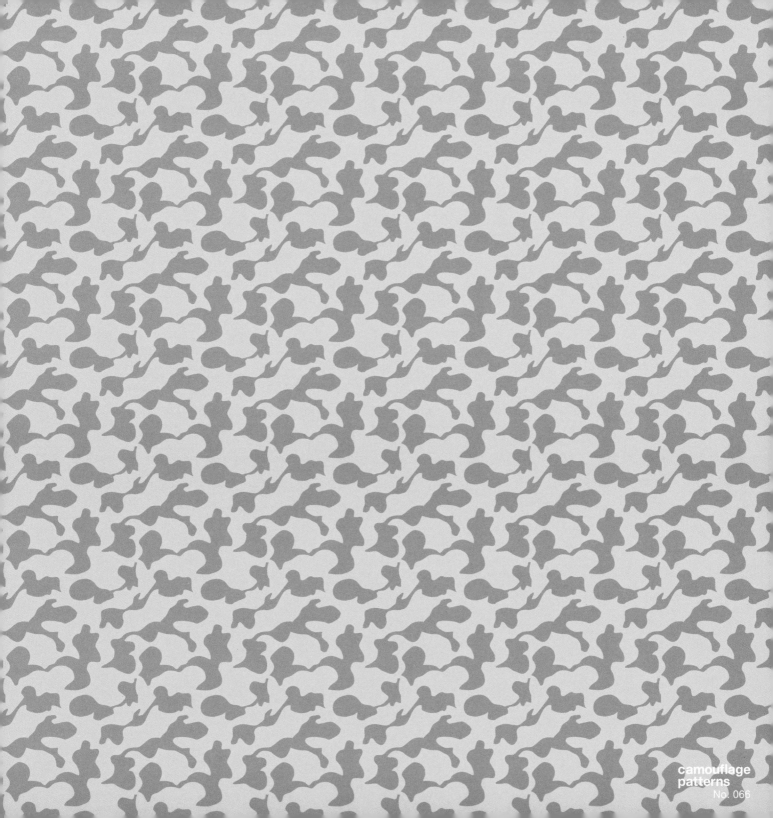

camouflage
patterns
No. 066

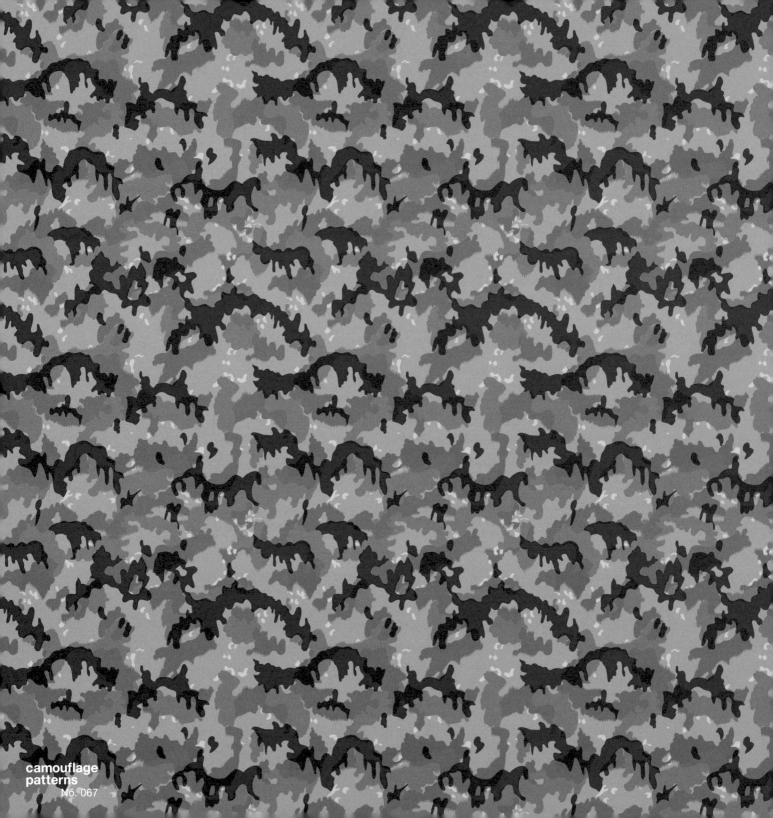

camouflage
patterns
No. 067

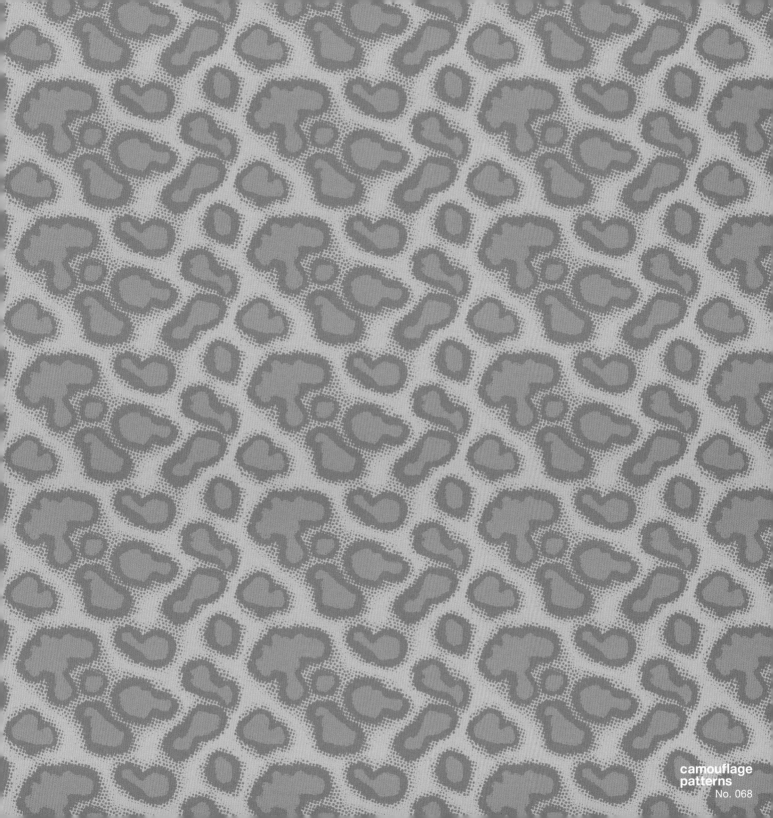

camouflage
patterns
No. 068

camouflage
patterns
No. 069

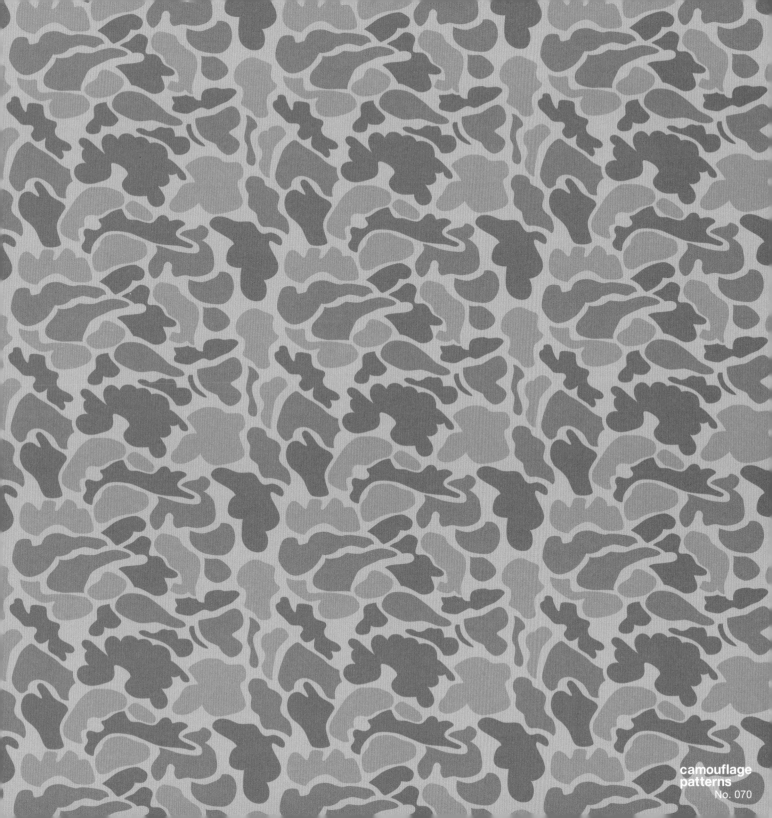

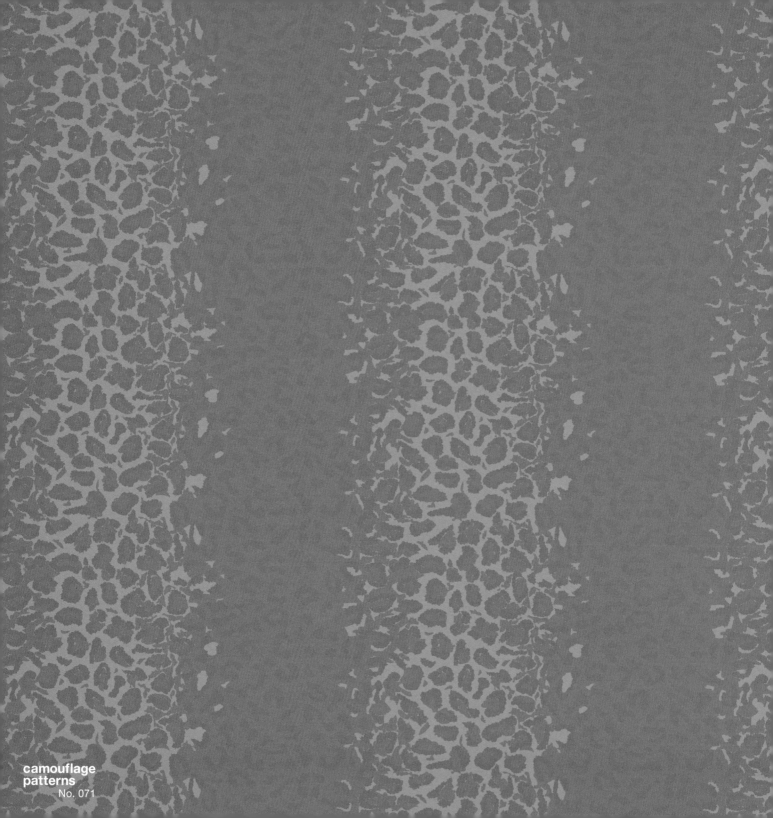

camouflage
patterns
No. 071

camouflage
patterns
No. 072

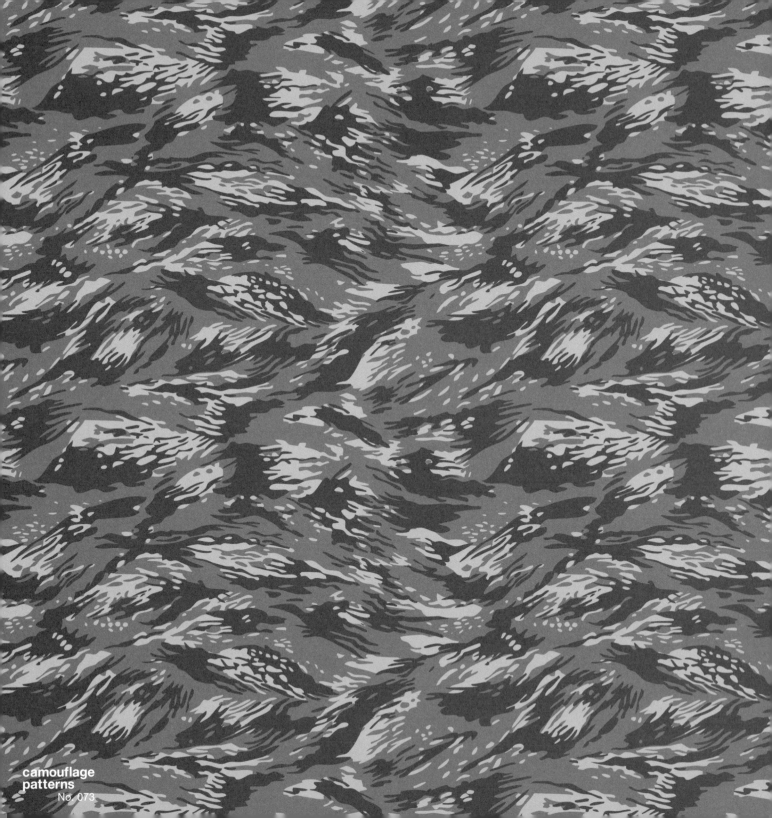

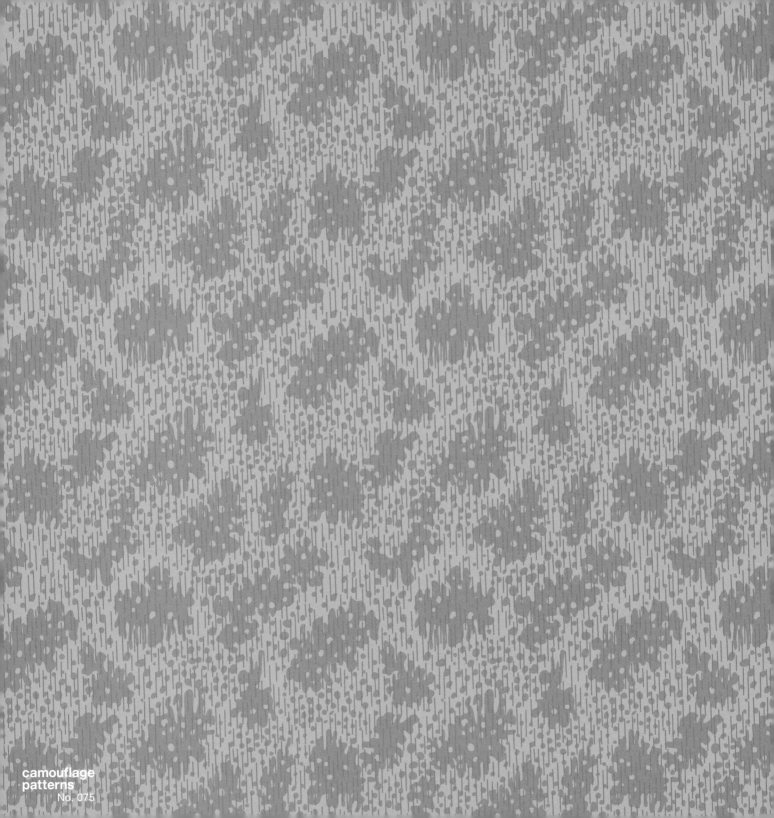

camouflage
patterns
No. 075

camouflage
patterns
No. 077

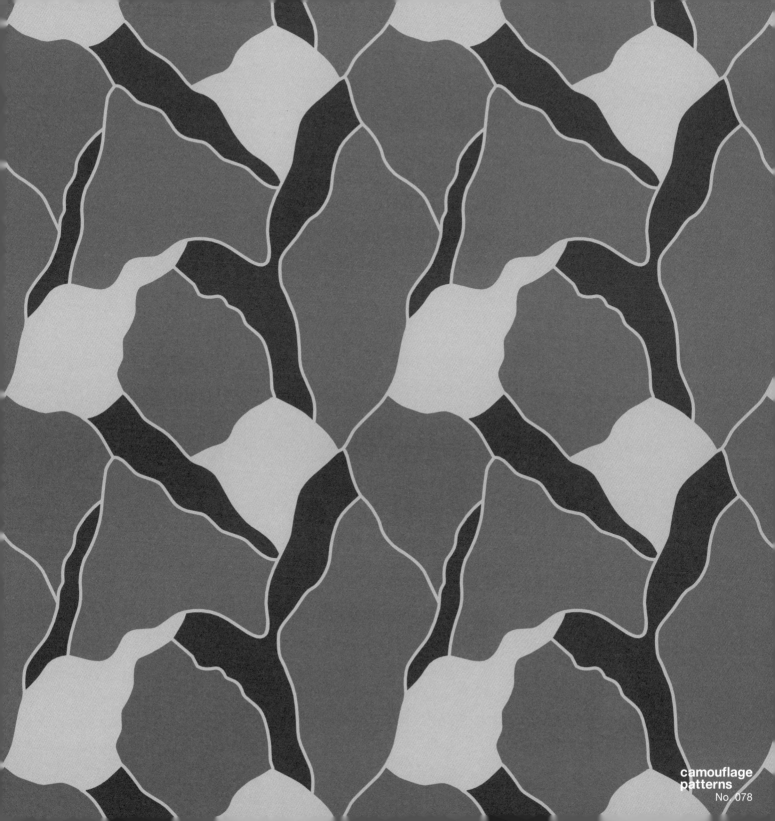

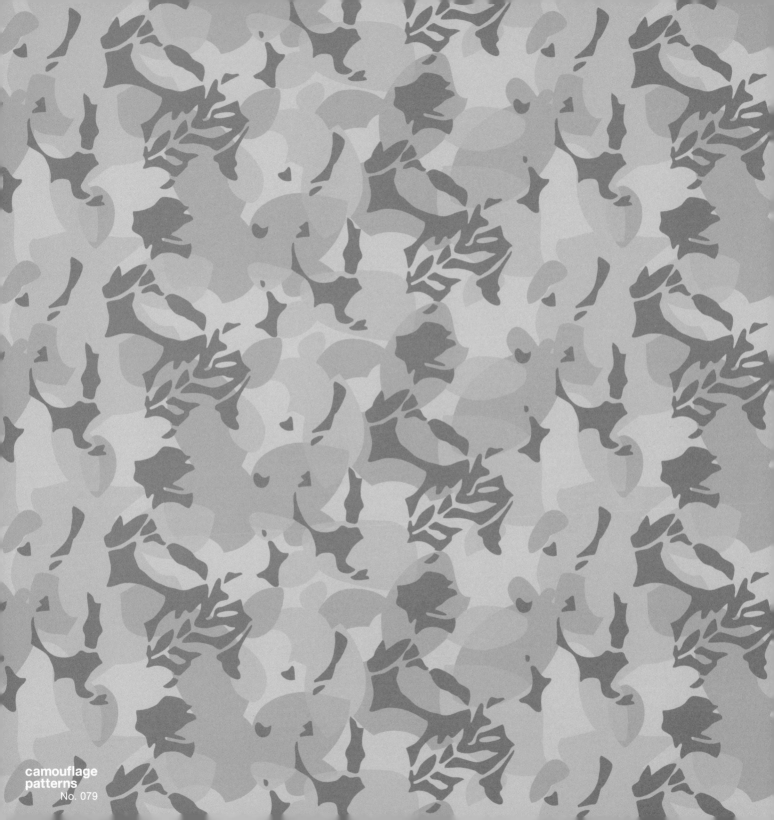

camouflage
patterns
No. 079

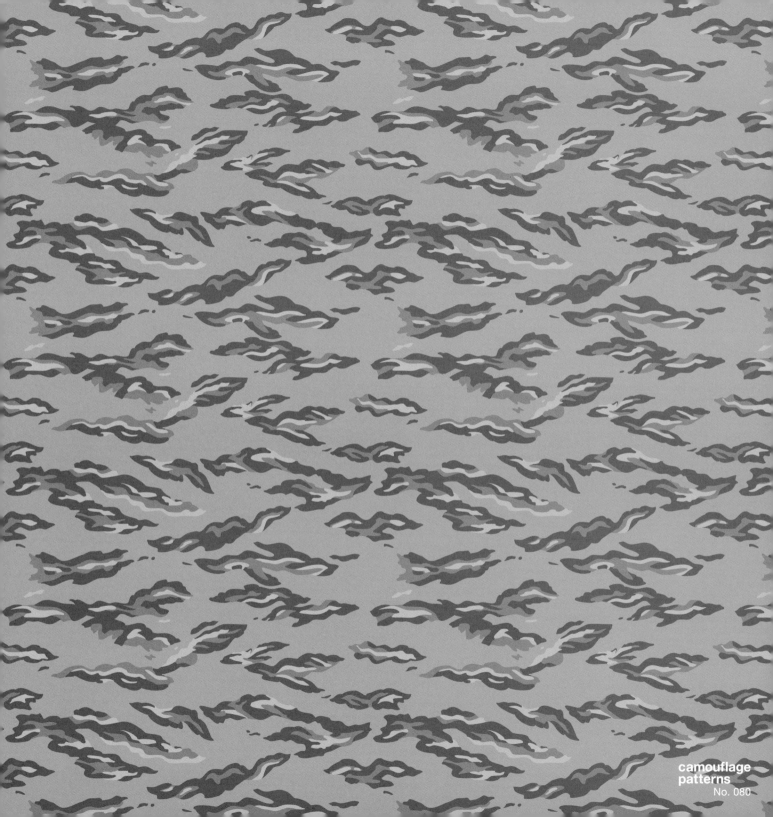

camouflage
patterns
No. 080

camouflage
patterns
No. 081

camouflage
patterns
No. 082

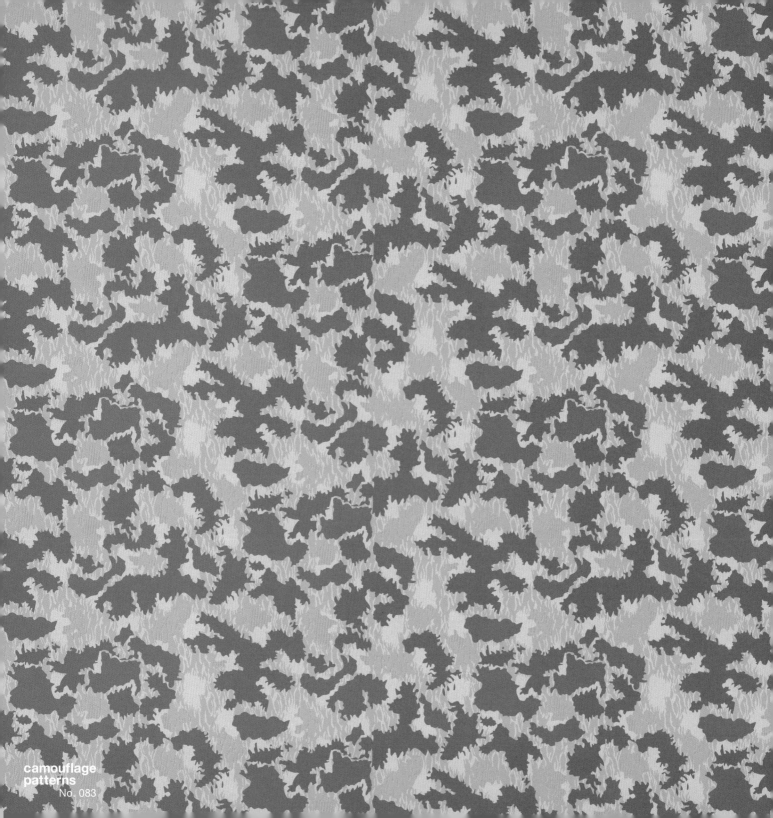

camouflage
patterns
No. 083

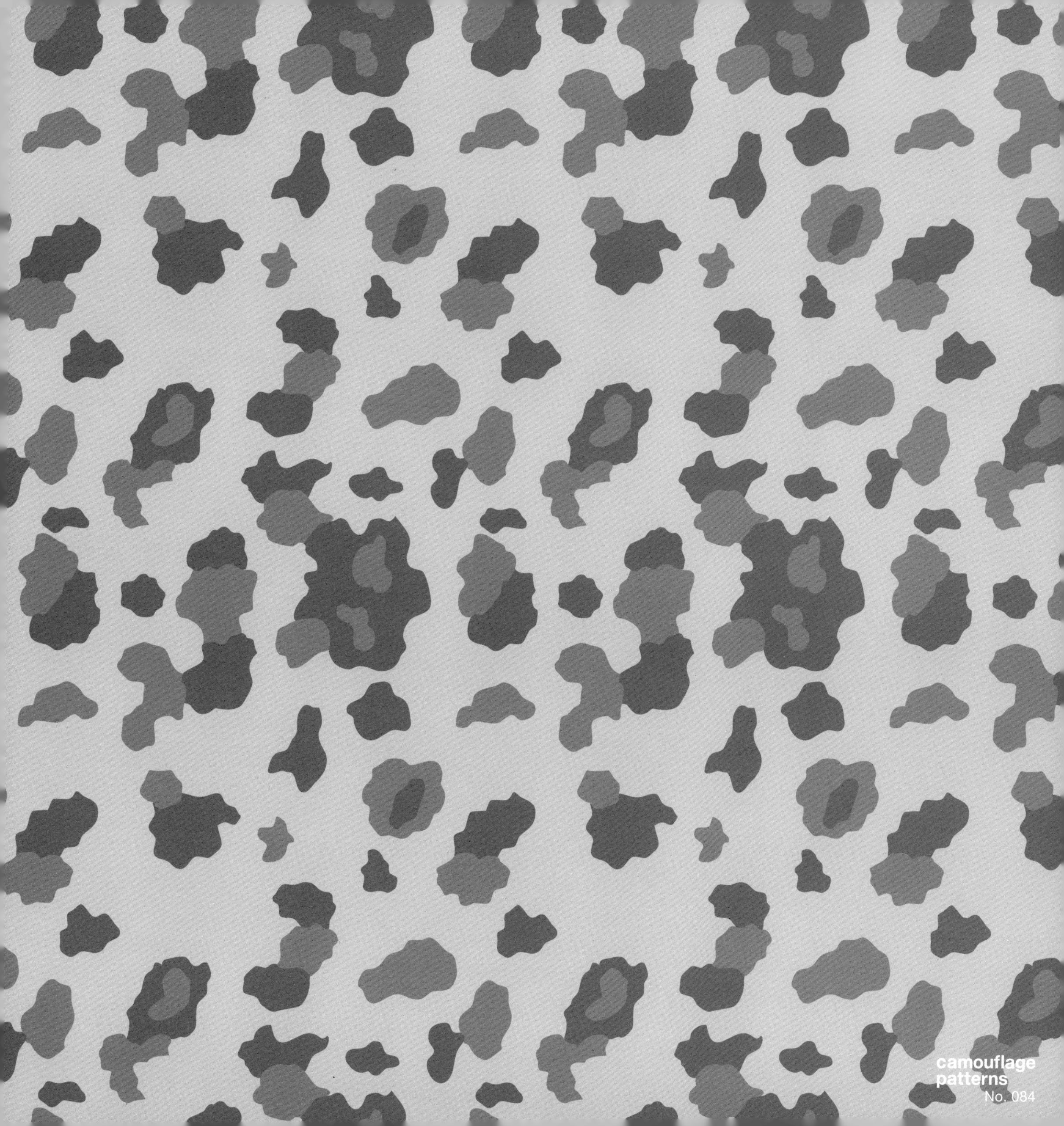
camouflage
patterns
No. 084

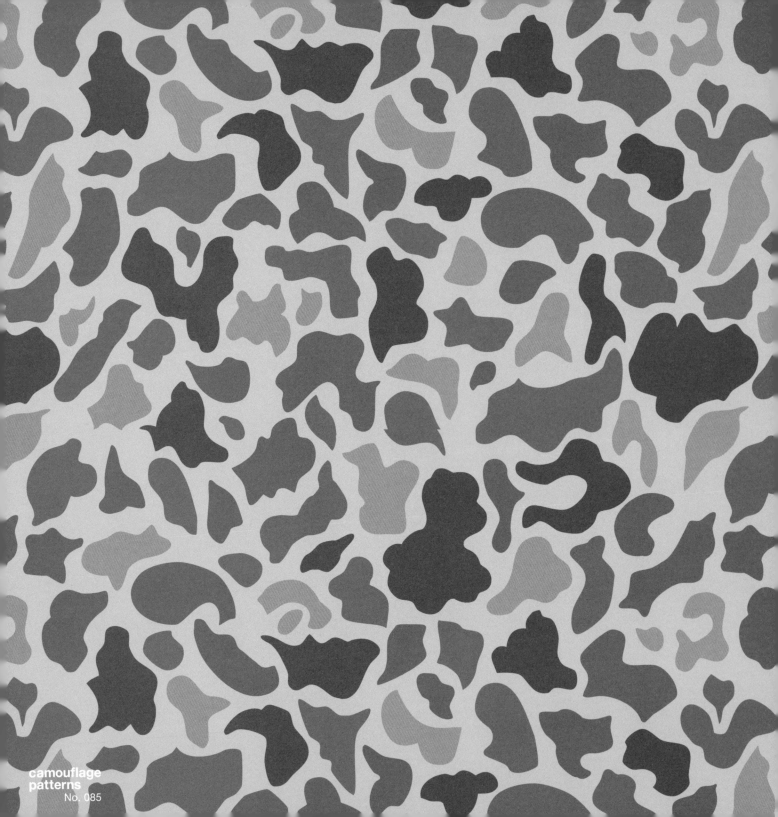

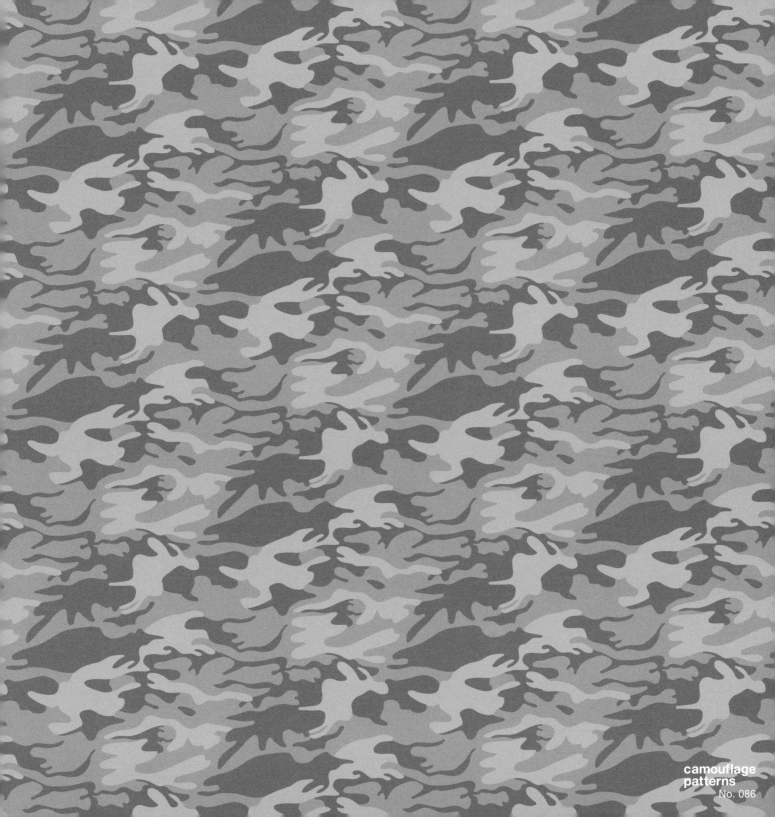

camouflage
patterns
No. 087

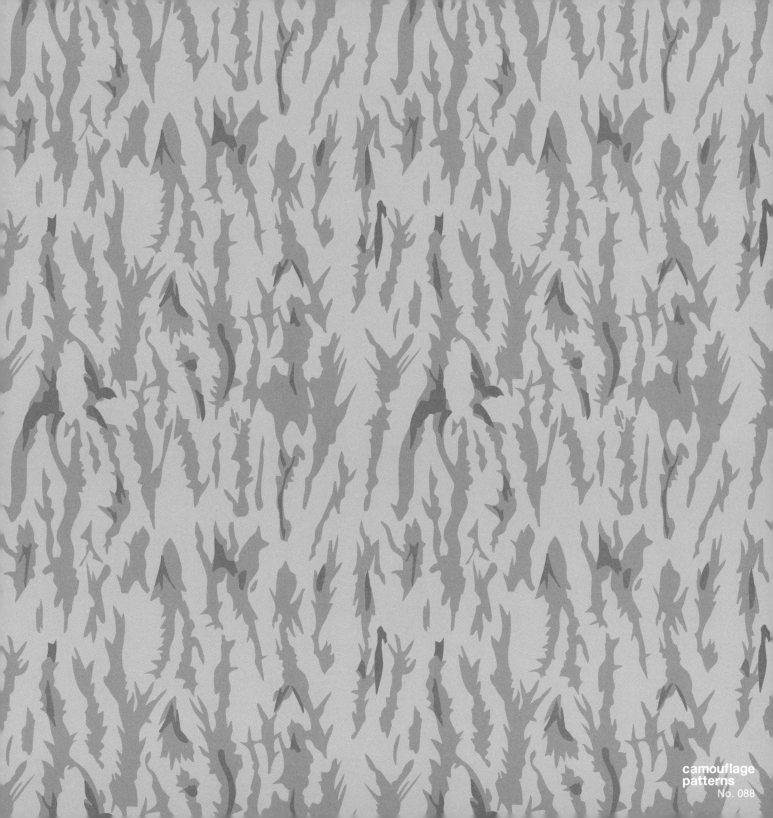

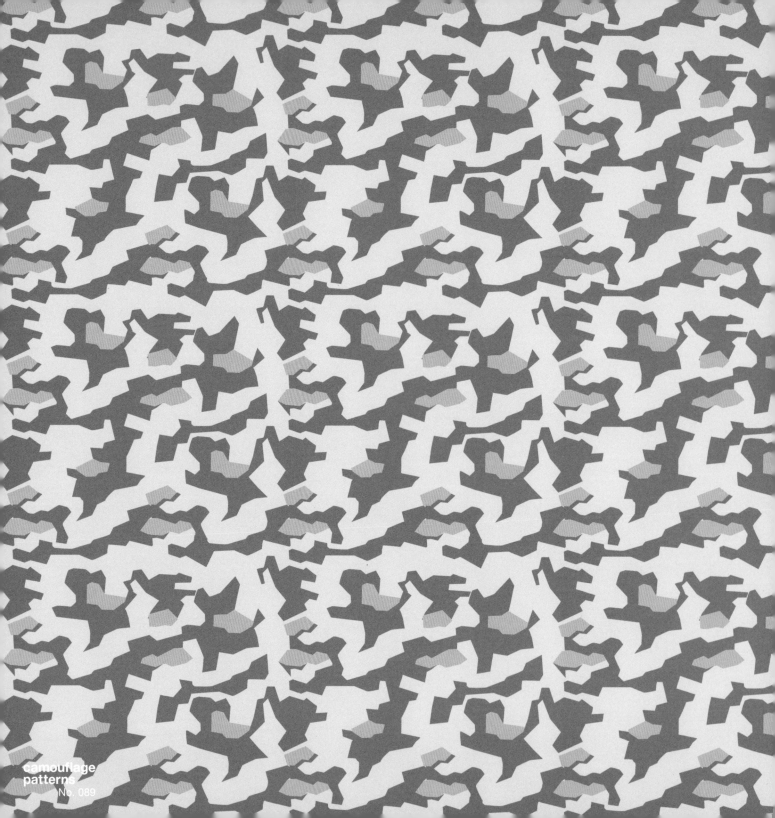

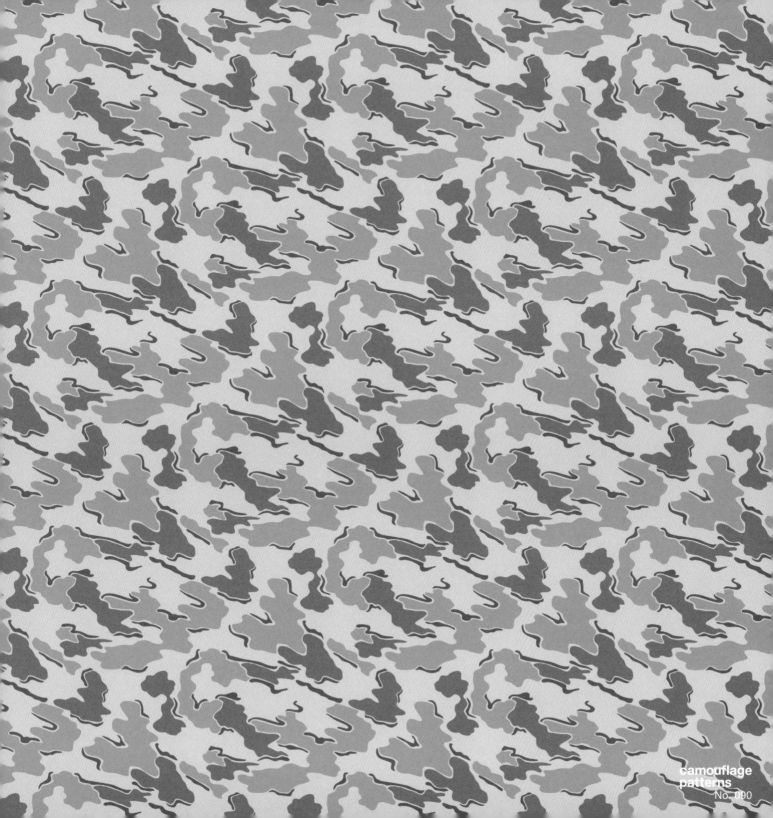

camouflage
patterns
No. 090

camouflage
patterns
No. 093

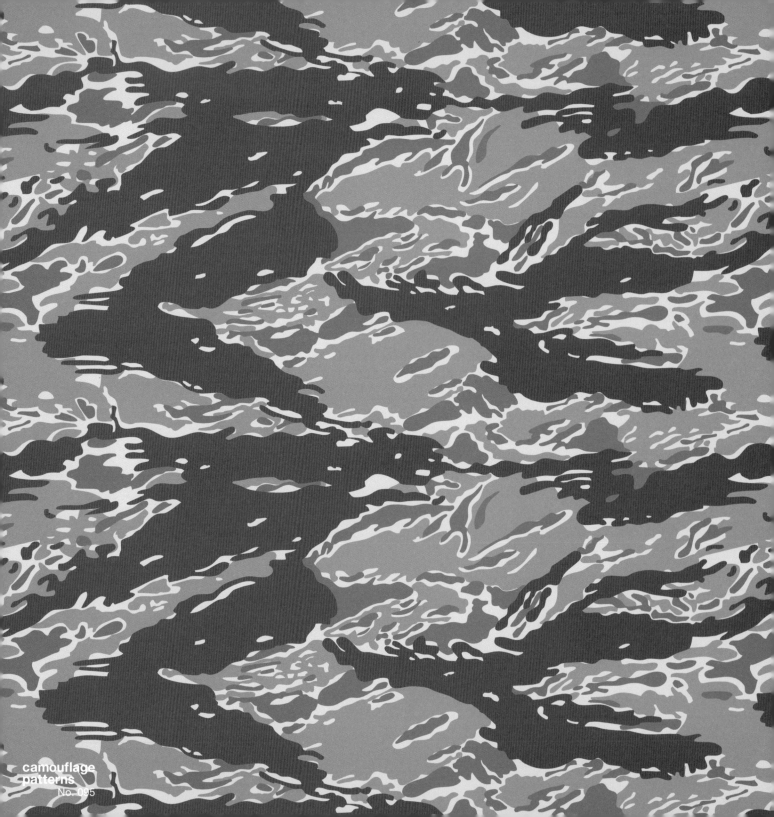

camouflage
patterns
No. 095

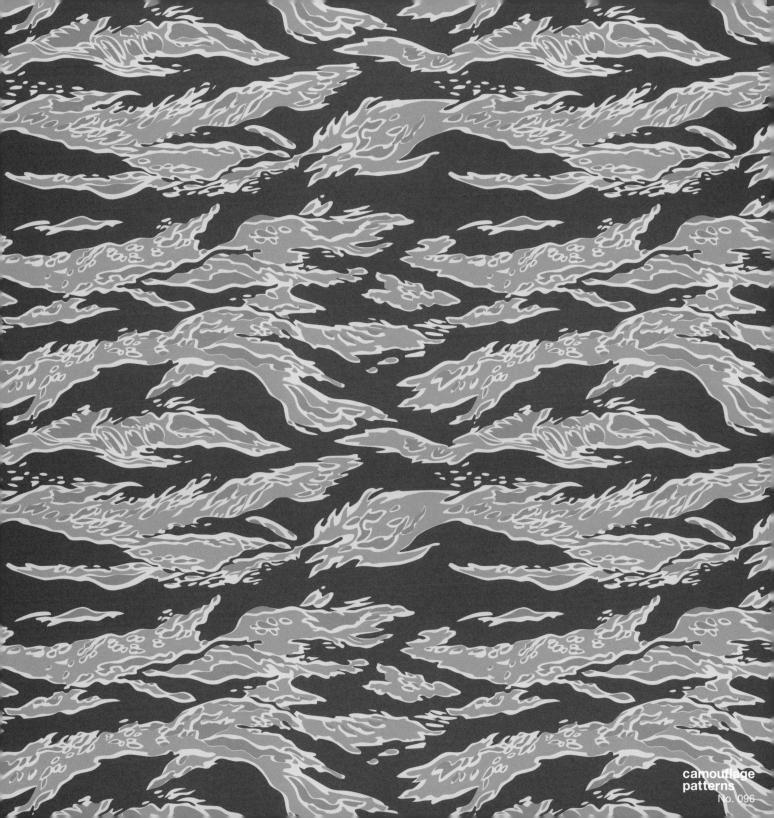

camouflage
patterns
No. 096

camouflage
patterns
No. 097

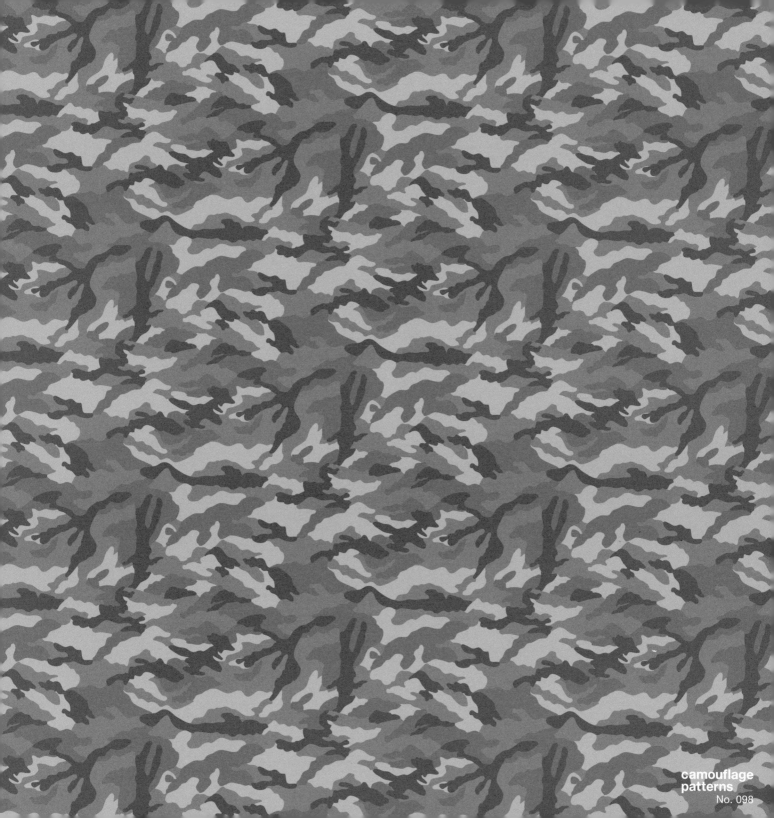

camouflage
patterns
No. 098

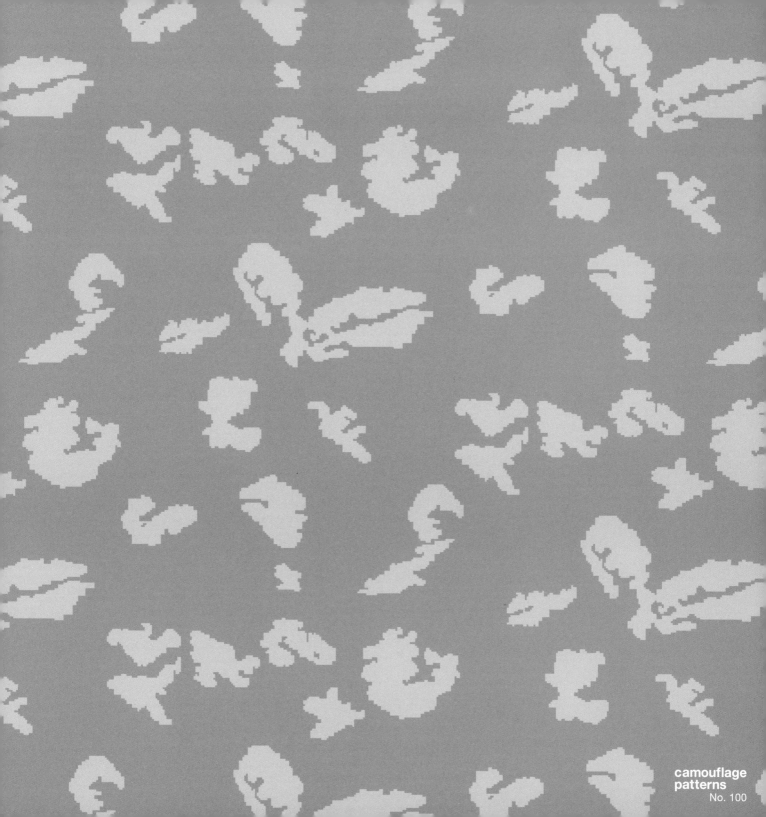

camouflage
patterns
No. 100

READ ME

5．責任の制限
弊社およびその供給者は、請求原因の如何を問わず、本ソフトウェアの使用または使用の不能および素材の利用から生じる全ての損害や不利益（利益の逸失およびデータの損壊を含む。）につき、一切責任を負わないものとします。

6．使用許諾の終了
ユーザーが本「camouflage patterns」CD-ROM使用許諾書に違反された場合は、弊社は、本「camouflage patterns」CD-ROM使用許諾書に基づくユーザーのライセンスを終了させることができます。

5. Limitation on Liability
DEX shall not be liable for any and all loss and disadvantage (inclusive of loss of profit and destruction of data) that may arise from the use or impossibility to use the Software and the use of the Materials irrespective of cause of a claim.

6. Termination of License
When the User has violated this Software License Agreement, DEX may terminate the license to the User under this License Agreement.

本製品に関するお問い合わせ先

● サポート・ダイアル［DEXサービスセンター］（本製品の操作上のお問い合わせ）
　 TEL：03-3980-0201　10：00～12：00，13：00～17：00　月曜日～金曜日（祝日を除く）
● ファックスによるお問い合わせ（インフォメーション、サポートとも共通）
　 FAX：03-5704-7351　24時間受付
〒153-0051 東京都目黒区上目黒2-9-35 中目黒GS第2ビル　　デザインエクスチェンジ株式会社

マルチユーザーライセンス・業務用ライセンス（商品化ライセンス）のお知らせ
弊社では、企業や団体など複数人で素材を御利用になるための「マルチユーザーライセンス」、またプリントショップや印刷業などで、サービスの一環として素材を利用していただくための「業務用ライセンス（商品化ライセンス）」それぞれを御用意しています。
「マルチユーザーライセンス」では、社内や部署内など、複数ライセンスを取得しなければならない状況において、利用する人数分のパッケージを購入していただくより便利な商品です。
「業務用ライセンス（商品化ライセンス）」では、ポストカードや印刷物の制作サービスで、お客様に直に素材を選んで御利用いただけるなど、サービスの付加価値がいっそう高まります。
どうぞ御利用くださいませ。
詳しくは、弊社ソリューションセールス営業部（TEL：03-5704-7357）までお問い合わせください。

Inquiry on the content of the CD-ROM to:

Fax: 81 3 5704 7354

E-mail: inti@dex.ne.jp

DesignEXchange Company Limited

Nakameguro GS Dai2 Bldg.
2-9-35 Kamimeguro
Meguro-ku Tokyo 153-0051 Japan

(To ensure the proper guidance to your inquiry, please help us to receive
the written messages only by fax or by e-mail.)

動作環境

■ 製品名 〔 camouflage patterns 〕

Windows
システム：Windows95 以上
メモリ：使用可能空きメモリ 8MB 以上
CD-ROM ドライブ
32000 色以上、640×480pic 以上のカラー表示が可能なモニタ
50MB 以上の HD の空き容量動作環境

Macintosh
システム：漢字 Talk7.5 以上
メモリ：使用可能メモリ 8MB 以上
CD-ROM ドライブ
32000 色以上、640×480pic 以上のカラー表示が可能なモニタ
50MB 以上の HD の空き容量

System requirement

■ camouflage patterns

Windows
OS: MS-Windows 95 or higher
RAM: 8MB or more
CD-ROM drive
Monitor: 32000 colors or more, 640 x 480 pixels or higher
Hard Disk: 50MB or more

Macintosh
OS: System 7.5 or higher
RAM: 8MB or more
CD-ROM drive
Monitor: 32000 colors or more, 640 x 480 pixels or higher
Hard Disk: 50MB or more

camouflage patterns

© 2002 DesignEXchange Company Limited

2002 年 3 月 31 日　初版第 1 刷発行
2002 年 10 月 31 日　初版第 2 刷発行

発行者　　　　　　大前正則
編集　　　　　　　GAS BOOK 編集部
アートディレクション　NENDO GRAPHIXXX
デザイン　　　　　C*2
ブックデザイン　　森泉勝也
英訳　　　　　　　リチャード・サドゥスキー ＋ 株式会社バベル
製作アシスタント　平田一晋
製作統括　　　　　駒野谷理子
印刷所　　　　　　大日本印刷株式会社
発行所　　　　　　デザインエクスチェンジ株式会社
　　　　　　　　　〒153-0051　東京都目黒区上目黒 2 丁目 9-35 中目黒 GS 第 2 ビル
　　　　　　　　　代表 TEL. 03-5704-7350
　　　　　　　　　代表 FAX. 03-5704-7351

ISBN 4-900852-90-2